Illustration Now!

PORTRAITS

Ed. Julius Wiedemann

Illustration Now!
PORTRAITS

TASCHEN

Contents
Inhalt/Sommaire

The Illustrated Portrait

by Julius Wiedemann

Artists have been making portraits since the very earliest times. In painting, portraiture is not only a genre, it is also an obligatory exercise for anyone who wants to become an artist. From my position as an editor, responsible for evaluating the work of hundreds of illustrators every year, the ability to draw well and to represent expressive faces is one of the first things I pay attention to, alongside a strong and mature stylistic visual language. Regardless of the technique used, the portrait artist is capable of depicting their object of study, telling a story, and going beyond the simple act of drawing a face. They thus portray the personality and the history of the person represented, giving the viewer the possibility of a deep and intimate look at the subject.

In illustration, the use of portraits has never been so important. Even with the wide availability of photography, the use of non-photographic portraits has gone far beyond the decision of simply being the last resource. Indeed, they have become an integral part of the story conveyed. Newspapers and magazines have without a doubt been among the heavy users of illustrated portraits, and have explored the form's possibilities to their maximum potential. The diversity of visual language offered today by many hundreds of illustrators, using a wide range of different techniques, provides us with a rich overview of people from the past and from our own times.

One of the most important institutions in the world for the genre, the National Portrait Gallery in London, was inaugurated in 1856 with the aim of documenting and preserving images of famous British men and women. It was only in 1969 that the Gallery started to accept images of living people, and 10 years later began to commission works for its own archive. Portraiture has thus become a way for us to look at the history of our society through images of its people. Today, there are hundreds of portrait galleries in museums all over the world, but comparatively few references in the market related to illustration. This book features the ways in which over 80 illustrators from around the world approach the art and craft of portraiture, with wide-ranging techniques, diverse visual languages, and numerous cultural backgrounds. We were also fortunate once again to have Steven Heller giving us a very insightful discussion of his views on the subject and the artists that make this work. We wish you an inspiring, colourful, and multi-faceted experience in the following pages.

← Portrait of Julius Wiedemann
by Kako, 2010; Adobe Illustrator,
Adobe Photoshop

Das illustrierte Porträt

von Julius Wiedemann

Schon seit frühester Zeit haben Künstler Porträts geschaffen. In der Malerei ist das Porträt nicht nur ein eigenes Genre, sondern auch eine obligatorische Disziplin für jeden angehenden Künstler. In meiner Funktion als Herausgeber, der jedes Jahr für die Einschätzung der Arbeiten Hunderter von Illustratoren verantwortlich ist, achte ich neben einer stilistisch starken und reifen visuellen Sprache zuerst auf die Fähigkeit, ausdrucksstarke Gesichter gut zeichnen und darstellen zu können. Ungeachtet der eingesetzten Technik ist der Porträtkünstler fähig, sein Studienobjekt abbilden und eine Geschichte erzählen zu können, und geht damit über den einfachen Akt der Zeichnung eines Gesichts hinaus. Der Künstler porträtiert Persönlichkeit und Geschichte der dargestellten Person und ermöglicht es dem Betrachter, einen tiefen und intimen Blick auf das Subjekt zu werfen.

In der Illustration war der Einsatz von Porträts nie so wichtig. Auch trotz der allgemeinen Verfügbarkeit der Fotografie ist der Einsatz nichtfotografischer Porträts längst nicht einfach mehr die letzte Zuflucht. Tatsächlich sind sie ein integraler Teil der übermittelten Geschichte. Zeitungen und Magazine gehören zweifellos zu den häufigsten Nutzern illustrierter Porträts und erforschen die Möglichkeiten dieser Form bis zu ihrem maximalen Potenzial. Die Diversität der visuellen Sprache, die heute von vielen Hunderten Illustratoren in einer großen Bandbreite unterschiedlichster Techniken geboten wird, liefert uns einen reichhaltigen Überblick über Menschen unserer Zeit und auch von früher.

Eine der weltweit wichtigsten Institutionen für dieses Genre ist die National Portrait Gallery in London, die 1856 feierlich eingeweiht wurde mit dem Ziel, Bilder berühmter britischer Frauen und Männer zu dokumentieren und zu erhalten. Erst seit 1969 ließ die Galerie Bilder von lebenden Persönlichkeiten zu, und zehn Jahre später begann sie, Arbeiten für ihr eigenes Archiv zu bestellen. Die Porträtmalerei ist somit für uns ein Weg, auf die Geschichte unserer Gesellschaft durch die Bilder ihrer Menschen zu schauen. Heute gibt es Hunderte von Porträtgalerien in Museen auf der ganzen Welt, aber vergleichsweise wenige Quellen auf dem Markt, die sich auf Illustrationen beziehen. In diesem Buch werden die vielen unterschiedlichen Herangehensweisen vorgestellt, wie sich mehr als 80 Illustratoren aus aller Welt mit breit gestreuten Techniken, vielfältigen visuellen Sprachen und zahlreichen kulturellen Hintergründen der Kunst und des Handwerks der Porträtmalerei widmen. Wir waren ebenfalls glücklich, dass Steven Heller uns wieder auf sehr aufschlussreiche Weise seine Ansichten zu diesem Thema und den Künstlern, die diese Arbeiten schaffen, erläutert. Wir wünschen Ihnen in der Beschäftigung mit den folgenden Seiten eine inspirierende und farbenprächtige Erfahrung voller vielfältigster Facetten.

Le portrait illustré

par Julius Wiedemann

Les artistes font des portraits depuis l'aube des temps. Dans la peinture, le portrait n'est pas seulement un genre, c'est aussi un exercice obligé pour quiconque veut devenir un artiste. En tant qu'éditeur, je suis responsable d'évaluer le travail de centaines d'illustrateurs chaque année, et l'une des premières choses que je recherche est la capacité à bien dessiner et à représenter des visages expressifs, ainsi qu'un langage visuel et stylistique fort et abouti. Quelle que soit la technique utilisée, l'artiste de portrait est capable de représenter l'objet de son étude en racontant une histoire, et en dépassant le simple acte de dessiner un visage. Il représente donc la personnalité et l'histoire de la personne, et donne au spectateur une perspective profonde et intime sur le sujet.

L'utilisation des portraits est plus importante que jamais dans l'illustration. Même si la photographie est un moyen extrêmement facile d'accès, l'utilisation de portraits non photographiques est bien loin d'être une solution de dernier recours. Ces portraits font en fait partie intégrante de l'histoire qui est racontée. Les journaux et magazines sont sans aucun doute parmi les plus grands consommateurs de portraits dessinés, et ont exploré les possibilités de cette forme jusqu'à exploiter à fond son potentiel. La diversité du langage visuel que des centaines et des centaines d'illustrateurs nous offrent aujourd'hui, avec un large éventail de techniques, nous donne un regard riche sur les acteurs de notre passé et de notre présent.

L'une des plus grandes institutions au monde pour ce genre, la National Portrait Gallery de Londres, a été inaugurée en 1856 dans le but de documenter et de préserver les images des Britanniques célèbres. Ce n'est qu'en 1969 que la Gallery a commencé à accepter des images représentant des personnes vivantes, et ce n'est que 10 ans plus tard qu'elle a commencé à commander des œuvres pour ses archives. Le portrait est donc devenu une façon de porter un regard sur l'histoire de notre société à travers la représentation de ses membres. Aujourd'hui, il y a des centaines de galeries de portraits dans les musées du monde entier, mais, en comparaison, peu de références sur le marché lié à l'illustration. Ce livre montre comment plus de 80 illustrateurs issus des quatre coins de la planète abordent l'art du portrait, avec des techniques, langages visuels et contextes culturels on ne peut plus variés. Nous avons aussi la chance de pouvoir profiter encore une fois des vues éclairées de Steven Heller sur le sujet et sur les artistes. Nous espérons que les pages qui suivent vous emmèneront dans un voyage plein d'inspiration, de couleurs et de diversité.

Portraiture Now: In Your (My) Face

by Steven Heller

I do not have a Facebook page but I do have an entire Facebook devoted just to me. A few years ago fifty illustrators created a small volume of portraits and caricatures of me, entitled *Facebook*, to commemorate a retrospective exhibition at The School of Visual Arts Gallery of my work. Each image was created in a different style, some were conceptual, others not. Many replicated me to a "t" while others were more abstractly interpretive and only faintly recognizable. I was truly touched by the artists' incredible generosity, however, dumbfounded by how I appeared through their eyes. Are my ears really that large (like Dumbo)? In my mind, I have always been Brad Pitt's identical twin! Most portraitees are not fond of their portraits.

Some of the drawings were very rigidly resolved, others were loose sketches, a few were 3D painted clay sculptures, and one was even made entirely out of yarn. There were, however, no photographs. Which leads me to ponder: why in this age of digital photography, when the average media consumer is so accustomed to seeing vivid, usually instantaneous, photos of personalities, is painted, drawn, and sculpted portraiture and caricature still popular enough to, well, fill this hefty book you are holding now?

The answer partially rests with art directorial preferences for illustration and photography that shift back and forth from time to time. Elaborate and expensive studio photography today dominates editorial and advertising, yet as the past three volumes of *Illustration Now!* clearly show, illustration is seen as an exuberant creative alternative that offers more personal, emotive and, at times, arresting imagery than a photograph. The overwhelming popular interest in celebrity has made personalities a major media commodity. So faces sell well.

While photographs sell decidedly more (and for more money) than illustration, the illustrated portrait, and especially caricature, is gaining in popularity – again. Rendered faces have long been a staple in publishing and advertising industries, as portraits invest an additional expressive layer – sometimes comedic or satirical, other times moody and emotive, and often iconic (in the graven image sense). Who doesn't know Milton Glaser's Sixties-era Dylan portrait or, more recently, Shepard Fairey's Obama "Hope" portrait. In addition, often a famous face is just so over-exposed that the illustrator's hand and eye inject a unique twist into a familiar pose.

Obviously, the face is the most recognizable part of our anatomy, more than stance, height or gait. Sometimes recognition is triggered by searing eyes, crooked mouth or jostled nose. Sometimes it is a mnemonic dimple or strange brow or even a mole. Often it is the hair that distinguishes you from me (especially me, since I don't have hair). But when all is said and done, the face – in whole or part – is the most challenging from the artist's perspective.

The question, what makes a good portrait? differs from artist to viewer to subject. Each has a subjective response. Yet in the art world a portrait can be almost anything that the artist says it is. "I do not paint a portrait to look like the subject," said Salvador Dalí, "rather does the subject grow to look like his portrait." The Futurist Umberto Boccioni added, "A portrait, to be a work of art, neither must nor may resemble the sitter… one must paint its atmosphere." Portraits are, therefore, a vehicle for expressing an artist's view – and in that sense a narcissistic activity. Really. An artist steals another's visage to represent his own. Try looking at portraits through that lens and see how different they appear.

With applied art – editorial and advertising – expression certainly may be a consequence but not an intent. Portraits and caricatures are intended first and foremost to convey information. If a pop star is portrayed it is because the story or advertisement being illustrated is about that pop star. The style may be conventional or raucous depending on the preference of the art director and manner of the artist, but the portrait serves a purpose: to illuminate the subject or theme. Even a caricature, which by definition embodies a personally critical or satirical point of view, is used for reasons other than pure expression. Caricatures are meant to be rude or crude or comic commentary on an individual.

The painter Francesco Clemente said he never paints a portrait from a photograph, "because a photograph doesn't give enough information about what the person feels." But most of the time, the illustrator must use photographs (scrap) to fulfill an assignment. Capturing inner feelings is a luxury and much less important than capturing the essential, albeit superficial, facial character. I can attest it is not easy – though easy to see when the result is labored or not. As an art director I spent many an uncomfortable moment with illustrators attempting to explain where a flawed portrait or caricature went wrong. What may look perfect to the illustrator misses in the eye of the beholder. This is as frequent in straight, representational portraiture as it is in cartoony caricature. With the former, copying the photographic reference too closely is usually as bad as not following it at all. With the latter, exaggerating the features too radically can eradicate any semblance of recognition. Balance is not the answer to the problem. There is no perfect balance or golden mean; it comes down to facility, skill, instinct – luck?

Some illustrators are born to be portraitists or caricaturists. They have the knack to rise above the common photorealist view to imbue a face with quirks and nuances that add a certain depth to the subject's character without it just being laid on for effect. While in good hands, there is nothing bad about creating special, stylistic effects – André Carrilho and Hanoch Piven do it so masterfully they enhance the viewing experience by adding vital biographical information, even feelings to their work – but exquisite portraiture enhances, as Dugald Stermer adeptly does, what nature has already bestowed without resorting to conceits.

Editors and advertisers once demanded that illustrators idealize the face and figure, thus codifying an aesthetic of universal beauty. In Western society this meant white, ethnically cleansed portraits of pretty or handsome models. Today faces come in the proverbial all shapes and sizes, styles and mannerisms, colors and hues. They seem to be more honest and arguably today's illustration is more in our face.

"The question, what makes a good portrait? differs from artist to viewer to subject. Each has a subjective response."

Porträts heute:
In Your (My) Face

von Steven Heller

Ich habe keine Facebook-Seite, aber ich besitze ein ganzes *Facebook*, das nur mir gewidmet ist. Vor ein paar Jahren schufen fünfzig Illustratoren einen kleinen Band mit Porträts und Karikaturen von mir und gaben ihm den Titel *Facebook*, um eine Retrospektive meiner Arbeiten an der School of Visual Arts Gallery zu würdigen. Jedes Bild wurde in einem anderen Stil kreiert, manche waren konzeptionell, andere nicht. Viele haben mich detailgenau repliziert, während andere eher abstrakt interpretierend und nur vage erkennbar waren. Ich war von der unglaublichen Großzügigkeit der Künstler wirklich gerührt, aber auch sprachlos darüber, wie ich in ihren Augen erschien. Habe ich wirklich so große Ohren wie Dumbo? Vor meinem geistigen Auge hielt ich mich immer für Brad Pitts eineiigen Zwilling! Nun, den meisten Porträtierten gefallen ihre Porträts nicht.

Einige der Zeichnungen waren sehr rigide ausgeführt, bei anderen handelte es sich um lockere Skizzen, ein paar waren bemalte dreidimensionale Lehmskulpturen, und ein Porträt war sogar ganz aus Garn gemacht. Es gab allerdings keine Fotografien. Das bringt mich ins Nachdenken: Warum ist in diesem Zeitalter der digitalen Fotografie, in der der durchschnittliche Medienkonsument so sehr daran gewöhnt ist, lebendige, meist sofort verfügbare Fotos von Persönlichkeiten zu sehen, die gemalte, gezeichnete oder bildhauerisch geformte Porträtkunst und Karikatur immer noch populär genug, um einen solch dicken Schmöker zu füllen, den Sie hier in Händen halten?

Zum Teil beruht die Antwort auf den Vorlieben des jeweiligen Art Director für Illustration und Fotografie, und diese Vorlieben verschieben sich gelegentlich. Aufwendige und kostspielige Studiofotografie dominiert heute den redaktionellen Teil und die Werbung, und doch – wie die früheren drei Bände von *Illustration Now!* eindeutig zeigen – wird Illustration als eine überschäumende Alternative betrachtet, die eine persönlichere, gefühlsbetontere und gelegentlich auch atemberaubendere Bildgebung ermöglicht als ein Foto.

Das überwältigende populäre Interesse an Prominenten hat Persönlichkeiten zu einem wichtigen medialen Erzeugnis gemacht. Also verkaufen sich Gesichter gut.

Während Fotografien entschieden mehr verkaufen als Illustrationen (und auch für mehr Geld), nimmt das illustrierte Porträt und vor allem die Karikatur (jetzt wieder) immer mehr an Popularität zu. Dargestellte Gesichter waren schon seit langem ein Grundbaustein in der Verlags- und Werbebranche, weil durch Porträts eine zusätzliche Ebene des Ausdrucks vermittelt werden kann – manchmal komisch oder satirisch, auch düster oder gefühlsbetont und oft symbolträchtig und ikonisch im Sinne eines Götzenbildes. Wer kennt nicht das Dylan-Porträt von Milton Glaser aus den Sechzigern oder als ein neueres Beispiel das „Hope"-Porträt von Obama, geschaffen von Shepard Fairey? Überdies wurden berühmte Gesichter bereits oft so übermäßig häufig dargestellt, dass der Illustrator mit seinem Blick und Geschick den vertrauten Posen noch einen überraschenden Aspekt abgewinnen kann.

Naheliegenderweise ist das Gesicht der am besten erkennbare Bereich unserer Anatomie, mehr als Haltung, Größe oder Gang. Manchmal lösen brennende Augen, ein verzogener Mund oder eine eingedrückte Nase das Erkennen aus. Manchmal dient ein Grübchen als Eselsbrücke oder eine eigenartig geformte Braue oder gar ein Leberfleck. Oft sind es die Haare, die den Unterschied bilden (vor allem bei mir, da ich keine habe). Doch letzten Endes ist aus künstlerischer Perspektive das Gesicht – entweder als Ganzes oder als Teil – die größte Herausforderung.

Die Frage, was ein gutes Porträt ausmacht, stellt sich unterschiedlich für Künstler, Betrachter und auch die Porträtierten. Alle haben ihre ganz persönliche Antwort darauf. Doch in der Welt der Kunst kann ein Porträt fast alles sein, zu dem der Künstler es erklärt. „Ich male kein Porträt, damit es wie der Porträtierte aussieht", sagte Salvador Dalí, „vielmehr wächst die porträtierte Person, damit sie wie das Porträt aussieht." Der Futurist Umberto Boccioni fügte

„Die Frage, was ein gutes Porträt ausmacht,
stellt sich unterschiedlich für Künstler, Betrachter
und auch die Porträtierten. Alle haben ihre
ganz persönliche Antwort darauf.“

hinzu: „Stellen wir noch einmal fest, dass ein Porträt, um ein Kunstwerk zu sein, seinem Modell weder ähnlich kann noch darf … seine Atmosphäre muss wiedergegeben werden.“ Porträts sind somit das Vehikel, mit dem der Künstler seine Sichtweise ausdrückt – und in diesem Sinne stellen sie eine narzisstische Aktivität dar. Wirklich, ein Künstler stiehlt das Gesicht eines anderen, um sein eigenes abzubilden. Versuchen Sie, Porträts durch diese Brille anzuschauen, und achten Sie darauf, wie unterschiedlich sie erscheinen.

Bei angewandter Kunst – im Editorial und bei der Werbung – ist Ausdruck vielleicht eine Konsequenz, aber nicht das Ziel. Porträts und Karikaturen sind zuallererst dazu gedacht, Informationen zu übermitteln. Wenn ein Popstar porträtiert wird, liegt das daran, dass die zu illustrierende Story oder Werbung von diesem Star handelt. Der Stil kann oder ungeschliffen sein – abhängig von den Präferenzen des Art Director und den Gepflogenheiten des Künstlers konventionell, doch das Porträt dient vornehmlich einem Zweck: Es soll das Subjekt oder Thema beleuchten. Sogar eine Karikatur, die per Definition einen persönlichen, kritischen oder satirischen Standpunkt verkörpert, wird aus anderen Gründen als dem reinen Ausdruck verwendet. Karikaturen sollen eine Person rüde, grell oder komisch kommentieren.

Der Maler Francesco Clemente sagte, dass er Porträts niemals nach Fotos malt, „weil ein Foto nicht genug Informationen darüber liefert, was die Person fühlt“. Doch meistens muss der Illustrator mit Fotografien ("Schnipsel") arbeiten, um einen Auftrag erfüllen zu können. Das Einfangen innerer Bewegungen und Gefühle ist ein Luxus und deutlich weniger wichtig als die wesentlichen, wenn auch oberflächlichen Gesichtszüge. Ich kann bezeugen, dass das nicht einfach ist – aber es ist deutlich zu erkennen, wenn das Resultat bemüht wirkt oder nicht. Als Art Director verbrachte ich so manchen unangenehmen Moment bei Illustratoren mit meinen Erklärungsversuchen, wo ein mangelhaftes Porträt oder eine Karikatur schief gegangen sei.

Was für den Illustrator perfekt aussieht, könnte dem Auge des Betrachters entgehen. Das geschieht in direkter, gegenständlicher Porträtmalerei genauso oft wie in cartoonhaften Karikaturen. Bei Ersterer ist es normalerweise ebenso schlecht, die fotografische Vorlage zu genau zu kopieren, wie ihr überhaupt nicht zu folgen. Bei Letzteren wird jede Ähnlichkeit oder jeder Wiedererkennungswert ganz ausgelöscht, wenn die Züge zu radikal übertrieben werden. Ausgewogenheit ist nicht die Antwort auf das Problem. Es gibt keine perfekte Balance oder goldene Mitte, es läuft letzten Endes auf Leichtigkeit, Geschick, Instinkt … und Glück? hinaus.

Manche Illustratoren sind geborene Porträtmaler oder Karikaturisten. Sie haben den Kniff heraus, den üblichen fotorealistischen Blick zu überwinden und ein Gesicht mit jenen kleinen Macken und Nuancen zu durchtränken, die dem Charakter des Subjekts eine gewisse Tiefe verleihen, ohne dass sie einfach nur als Effekt aufgesetzt werden. Kommt das aus guten Händen, ist nichts daran auszusetzen, spezielle stilistische Effekte zu schaffen (André Carrilho und Hanoch Piven machen das ganz meisterhaft, indem sie ihre Arbeiten um wesentliche biografische Informationen und sogar Gefühle ergänzen und somit das Erlebnis des Betrachters erweitern), doch eine exquisite Porträtmalerei, so wie sie meisterhaft von Dugald Stermer vorgeführt wird, erweitert das bereits von der Natur Geschenkte, ohne auf Einbildungen zurückgreifen zu müssen.

Von Herausgebern und Werbeleuten wurde mal eingefordert, Illustratoren sollten Gesicht und Statur idealisieren und somit eine Ästhetik der universellen Schönheit kodifizieren. In der westlichen Welt bedeutete das die Darstellung von weißen, ethnisch gereinigten Porträts gutaussehender oder attraktiver Modelle. Heutige Gesichter erscheinen im wahrsten Sinne des Wortes in allen Formen und Größen, Stilen und Eigenarten, Farben und Nuancen. Sie erscheinen ehrlicher, und die heutigen Illustrationen dürften uns wohl viel eher gut zu Gesicht stehen.

Le portrait aujourd'hui : In Your (My) Face

par Steven Heller

Je n'ai pas de compte sur Facebook, mais j'ai tout un *Facebook* consacré à moi, et à moi seul Il y a quelques années, cinquante illustrateurs ont créé un petit ouvrage composé de portraits et de caricatures de moi, intitulé *Facebook*, à l'occasion d'une exposition rétrospective de mon œuvre à la School of Visual Arts Gallery. Chaque image avait un style différent ; certaines étaient conceptuelles, d'autres non. Beaucoup me représentaient fidèlement, mais d'autres étaient des interprétations plus abstraites, et j'y étais à peine reconnaissable. L'incroyable générosité des artistes m'a beaucoup touchée, mais je suis resté perplexe devant la façon dont ils me voyaient. Mes oreilles sont-elles vraiment aussi grandes (comme Dumbo) ? Dans mon esprit, j'ai toujours été le jumeau de Brad Pitt ! La plupart des gens n'aiment pas les portraits que l'on fait d'eux.

Certains ont été exécutés avec une grande rigueur, d'autres étaient des ébauches très libres, quelques-uns étaient des sculptures en argile en 3D, et l'un d'eux était même réalisé entièrement en fil. Mais il n'y avait pas une seule photographie. Ce qui m'amène à me demander : pourquoi, à l'ère de la photographie numérique, alors que le consommateur de médias moyen est si habitué à voir des photos de célébrités détaillées et généralement instantanées, les portraits et caricatures sous forme de dessins, peintures et sculptures sont-ils encore assez populaires pour remplir le volume imposant que vous tenez entre vos mains ?

La réponse se trouve en partie dans la préférence que les directeurs artistiques donnent à l'illustration ou à la photographie, et qui change selon le moment. Aujourd'hui, les photographies de studio sophistiquées et coûteuses dominent l'édition et la publicité, et pourtant, comme le montrent clairement les trois derniers volumes d'*Illustration Now!*, l'illustration est considérée comme une autre possibilité créative extrêmement riche qui propose des images plus personnelles, plus émotives et, parfois, plus saisissantes que la photographie. L'énorme intérêt que le public porte

aux célébrités en a fait une marchandise de choix pour les médias. Les visages vendent.

Les photographies vendent nettement mieux (et plus cher) que les illustrations, mais les portraits sous forme d'illustration, et particulièrement les caricatures, ont un regain de popularité. Les visages dessinés ont longtemps été un composant de base dans l'édition et la publicité, car les portraits apportent un élément expressif supplémentaire – parfois humoristique ou satirique, parfois sombre et émotif, et souvent emblématique. Qui n'a jamais vu le portrait de Dylan que Milton Glaser a réalisé dans les années soixante ou, plus récemment, le portrait « Hope » d'Obama par Shepard Fairey ? Sans compter que, souvent, un visage célèbre est tout simplement tellement connu que la patte et le regard de l'illustrateur injectent de la nouveauté dans le familier.

Évidemment, le visage est la partie la plus reconnaissable de notre anatomie, bien plus que la posture, la taille ou la démarche. Parfois, cette reconnaissance est déclenchée par un regard perçant, une bouche tordue ou un nez accidenté. Parfois c'est une fossette qui se grave dans la mémoire, ou un sourcil étrange, ou même un grain de beauté. Ce sont souvent les cheveux qui nous distinguent (surtout pour moi, puisque je n'en ai pas). Mais en fin de compte, le visage – tout ou partie – est l'élément le plus difficile à traiter pour un artiste.

Ce qui fait un bon portrait est une question qui dépend de l'artiste, du spectateur et du sujet. Chacun a une réponse subjective. Pourtant, dans le monde de l'art, un portrait peut être pratiquement n'importe quoi, du moment que l'artiste dit que c'est un portrait. « Je ne peins pas un portrait pour qu'il ressemble à son sujet », a dit Salvador Dalí, « c'est plutôt le sujet qui finit par ressembler à son portrait ». Le futuriste Umberto Boccioni a ajouté : « Un portrait, pour être une œuvre d'art, ne doit ni ne peut ressembler au modèle… c'est son atmosphère qu'il faut peindre. » Les portraits sont donc le véhicule de l'expression de la vision de l'artiste,

*« Ce qui fait un bon portrait est une question
qui dépend de l'artiste, du spectateur et du sujet.
Chacun a une réponse subjective. »*

et en ce sens, il s'agit d'une activité narcissique. Vraiment. Un artiste vole le visage de quelqu'un d'autre pour représenter le sien propre. Essayez de regarder les portraits à travers ce prisme, et vous ne les verrez plus de la même manière.

Dans les arts appliqués – l'édition et la publicité – l'expression peut sans doute être une conséquence, mais pas une intention. Les portraits et les caricatures ont pour mission première et principale de transmettre des informations. Le portrait d'une pop star n'est là que parce qu'un article ou une publicité est publié à propos de cette pop star. Il peut être classique ou excentrique, selon les préférences du directeur artistique et le style de l'artiste, mais le portrait a une mission : apporter un éclairage sur le sujet ou le thème. Même une caricature, qui par définition représente un point de vue personnel satirique ou critique, est utilisée pour des raisons différentes de la pure expression. Les caricatures sont censées être un commentaire impoli, grossier ou humoristique à propos d'une personne.

Le peintre Francesco Clemente a dit qu'il ne peignait jamais un portrait d'après photographie, « parce qu'une photographie de donne pas assez d'informations sur ce que la personne ressent ». Mais la plupart du temps, l'illustrateur doit utiliser des photographies pour faire son travail. Saisir des émotions est un luxe, et est bien moins important que saisir le caractère du visage, bien qu'il soit plus superficiel. Je peux confirmer que ce n'est pas facile – mais qu'il est facile de voir si le résultat est réussi ou non. En tant que directeur artistique, j'ai passé de nombreux moments inconfortables avec des illustrateurs, à leur expliquer en quoi un portrait ou une caricature n'était pas satisfaisant. Ce qui peut sembler parfait à un illustrateur peut aussi manquer son but au regard du spectateur. C'est tout aussi fréquent dans les portraits classiques, fidèles au sujet, que dans la caricature humoristique. Pour les portraits classiques, copier la référence photographique trop fidèlement est généralement aussi mauvais que de ne pas la suivre du tout. Pour les caricatures, une exagération

trop radicale des traits peut éliminer toute ressemblance. L'équilibre n'est pas la solution. Il n'y a pas d'équilibre parfait, ni de règle d'or. Il s'agit plutôt de facilité, de talent, d'instinct – de chance ?

Certains illustrateurs sont nés pour être portraitistes ou caricaturistes. Ils ont le don de dépasser la vision réaliste courante et de révéler les bizarreries et les nuances d'un visage pour ajouter une certaine profondeur au caractère du sujet, en évitant toute artificialité. Pour un bon artiste, ce n'est pas un problème de créer des effets spéciaux de style – André Carrilho et Hanoch Piven le font si magistralement qu'ils subliment le résultat en ajoutant des informations biographiques ou même des émotions à leur œuvre – mais les meilleurs portraits soulignent, comme Dugald Stermer le fait avec talent, ce que la nature a déjà accordé sans avoir recours à des artifices.

À une époque, les éditeurs et les publicitaires demandaient aux illustrateurs d'idéaliser le visage et la silhouette, codifiant ainsi une esthétique de la beauté universelle. Dans la société occidentale, cela s'est traduit par des portraits de modèles physiquement irréprochables, blancs, sans appartenance ethnique. Aujourd'hui, les visages embrassent tout le spectre de la diversité, et sont représentés dans tous les styles et toutes les couleurs. Ils semblent plus honnêtes, et l'illustration moderne avance à visage découvert.

Portrait
ILLUSTRATORS
from A to Z

← Portrait of Bayard Rustin by
Dugald Stermer, 2002, *Los Angeles Times*,
magazine article; hand drawing, pencil,
watercolour on Arches watercolour paper

Henrik Abrahams

lives and works in Berlin, Germany
www.henrikabrahams.com

AGENT
VO Valérie Oualid
France
www.valerieoualid.com

*"Faces tell stories,
and if it's a good story,
it's a pleasure to tell
that in my language."*

„Gesichter erzählen Geschichten,
und wenn es eine gute Geschichte
ist, wird es zum Genuss, sie in meiner
Sprache zu erzählen."

« Les visages racontent des histoires,
et si l'histoire est bonne, c'est un plaisir
de la raconter dans mon propre langage. »

↑   Werner Bergengruen, 2009,
personal work; mixed media

→   *One*, 2010, My World Is, T-shirt;
mixed media

→→ *Komm zurück*, 2010, *Das Magazin*,
magazine cover; mixed media

↑   Jens Uehlecke, 2010, *Zeit Wissen*,
editorial; mixed media

→   *Forscher gesucht*, portrait of
Elinor Ostrom, 2010, *Zeit Wissen*,
editorial; mixed media

→→ *Claudia*, 2010, *Zeit Wissen*,
editorial; mixed media

←   *Keine Angst vorm schwarzen Mann*,
portrait of Andreas Sentker, 2010,
Zeit Wissen, editorial; mixed media

Jorge Alderete

lives and works in Mexico City, Mexico
www.jorgealderete.com

AGENT

Pocko
London
www.pocko.com

Vertigo
Mexico
www.vertigogaleria.com

"My relationship with 'the portrait' changes substantially for me when the portrayed person ceases to be an unknown person, and becomes someone in my immediate surroundings."

„*Meine Beziehung zum ‚Porträt' verändert sich grundsätzlich, wenn die porträtierte Person nicht mehr unbekannt ist. Dann wird sie zu jemandem aus meiner unmittelbaren Umgebung.*"

«*Ma relation au ‹ portrait › change substantiellement pour moi lorsque la personne représentée cesse d'être inconnue, et devient quelqu'un qui s'inscrit dans mon environnement immédiat.*»

↑ Los Fabulosos Cadillacs, 2008, Sony BMG, CD cover; digital

→→ *Capitalist China*, portrait of Mao Tse-Tung, 2005, *Deep*, magazine article; digital

JORGE.ALDERETE.COM

EL DOLIENTE HIDALGO // **DR. ALDERETE** // WWW.JORGEALDERETE.COM

←← *El Doliente Miguel Hidalgo*, portrait of Miguel Hidalgo, 2010, Bicentenario Pop exhibition, poster; digital

→ Jorge Alderete, self-portrait, 2008, Black Cat Bones, personal work, exhibition; silkscreen over used poster

↘ *Tranquilino Yokosuna*, portrait of Arturo Tranquilino, 2008, Black Cat Bones, personal work, exhibition; silkscreen over used poster

↓ Gaby Enterradores, 2008, Black Cat Bones, personal work, exhibition; silkscreen over used poster

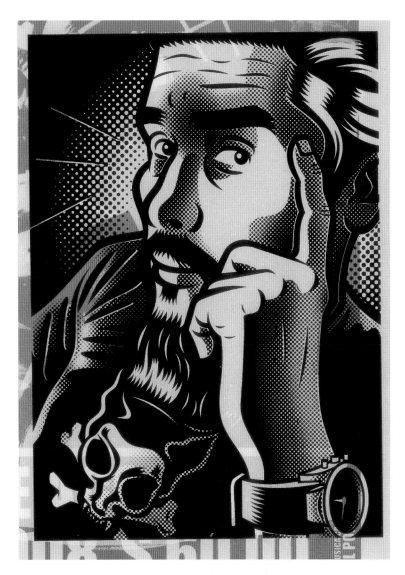

↑   Gary Panter, 2009, *Replicante*,
magazine article; digital

→   *Shigeo Fukuda Homage*, portrait
of Shigeo Fukuda, 2009, International
Biennial of the Poster in Bolivia,
poster; digital

→→ *La Mano de Dios*, portrait of
Diego Armando Maradona, 2010,
Football Heroes, book; digital

Jorge Arévalo

lives and works in Madrid, Spain
www.jorgearevalo.com

"*I always try to get to the character and his expression with the fewest strokes possible, synthesising the faces as much as possible and contrasting voluptuous textures with clean strokes.*"

„*Ich versuche stets, mit möglichst wenigen Strichen Charakter und Ausdruck einzufangen, wobei ich das Gesicht so gut aufbaue wie möglich und üppige Texturen zu klaren Strichen in Kontrast setze.*"

«*J'essaie toujours de capturer le personnage et son expression avec le moins de traits possible, en synthétisant les visages autant que possible et en créant un contraste entre des textures voluptueuses et des traits nets.*»

↑   Miles Davis, 2009, *Vanity Fair*, magazine article; Adobe FreeHand, hand drawing

→→ Amy Winehouse, 2009, *Retratos 2*, book; Adobe FreeHand, hand drawing

↑   Anthony Hopkins, 2009, *El Mundo*,
newspaper article; Adobe FreeHand

↗   Michael Caine, 2008, *El Mundo*,
Metropoli, magazine article;
Adobe FreeHand, hand drawing

← Nat King Cole, 2009,
Retratos 2, book; Adobe FreeHand

↓ Juliette Binoche, 2008,
El Mundo, *Metropoli*, magazine article;
Adobe FreeHand, hand drawing

↑ Elijah Wood, 2008, *El Mundo*,
Metropoli, magazine article;
Adobe FreeHand, hand drawing

←← Audrey Tautou, 2008, *El Mundo*,
Metropoli, magazine article;
Adobe FreeHand, hand drawing

Lisel Ashlock

lives and works in New York (NY), USA
www.liseljane.com

AGENT
The Loud Cloud
www.theloudcloud.com

> *"There is nothing more satisfying in image making than looking at the face as an object, and deconstructing its complexity line by line."*

> *„Beim Malen eines Bildes gibt es nichts, was einen mehr befriedigt, als das Gesicht als Objekt zu betrachten und seine Komplexität Linie um Linie zu dekonstruieren."*

> *« Il n'y a rien de plus satisfaisant dans la création d'images que de voir le visage comme un objet, et de déconstruire sa complexité ligne par ligne. »*

↑   *Cathy/Kate of East of Eden*, 2009, personal work; acrylic and pencil on birch panel

→   Stonewall Jackson, 2009, personal work; acrylic and pencil on birch panel

→→ Jacques Cousteau, 2010, commission; acrylic and pencil on birch panel

↑ Scheherazade of *Martin Amis'*
The Pregnant Widow, 2010, *Playboy*;
acrylic and pencil on birch panel

←← Viggo Mortensen in the movie
The Road, 2009, *Gentleman's Quarterly*;
acrylic and pencil on birch panel

↑ Sigmund Freud, 2009, personal work;
acrylic and pencil on birch panel

←← Carl Sagan, 2010, personal work;
acrylic and pencil on birch panel

Christian Barthold

lives and works in Cologne, Germany
www.myspace.com/artmancologne

*"In my portraits, I am a traveller
in different styles."*

*„In meinen Porträts reise ich durch
verschiedene Stile."*

*« Dans mes portraits, je voyage
entre différents styles. »*

↑ *Entdeckung der Röntgenstrahlen*,
portrait of Wilhelm Röntgen, German
physicist, 2008, Campus Verlag, book;
acrylic on paper

→ *My very beautiful Mother*, portrait
of Elke Barthold, 2009, personal work;
acrylic and collage on woodboard

→→ *100 Tage Schwarz-Gelb*, portrait of
Angela Merkel and Guido Westerwelle,
2009, *Die Tageszeitung*, newspaper article;
acrylic and collage on woodboard

↑   *Bassplayer*, 2010, personal work;
Japico ink on cheap paper

→   *Saxman*, 2009, personal work;
Japico ink on cheap paper

→→ *Handy Man*, 2009, personal work;
Japico ink on cheap paper

Sarah Beetson

lives and works in Gold Coast (Queensland), Australia
www.sarahbeetson.com

AGENT

Illustration Ltd
London
www.illustrationweb.com

i2i Art Inc
Toronto
www.i2iart.com

19 Karen Contemporary
Artspace, Australia
www.19karen.com.au

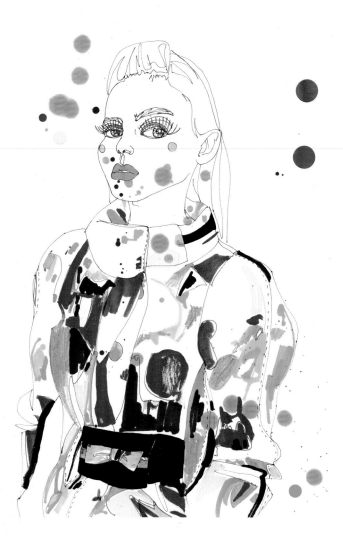

"I am always preoccupied with the politics and perversities of popular culture, who we are as a collective society, and the subjects that lurk beneath the surface."

„Stets bin ich mit dem Treiben und den Perversitäten der populären Kultur beschäftigt, wer wir als kollektive Gesellschaft sind und welche Themen unter der Oberfläche lauern."

« Je suis toujours préoccupée par la politique et les perversités de la culture populaire, notre identité en tant que société collective, et les sujets tapis sous la surface. »

↑   *Erdem Fall 08 Ready To Wear*, portrait of model backstage at Erdem, 2008, British Fashion Council; mixed media on paper, pens, tissue paper, gouache, acrylic, markers, collage

→   Sarah Beetson, self-portrait, 2009, Perth Fashion Week, Western Australian Government; mixed media on paper, pens, tissue paper, gouache, acrylic, markers, collage

→→ *Black Martini*, portrait of Dyana Gray, 2008, Bajo El Alma Boutique, Uruguay; mixed media on paper, pens, tissue paper, gouache, acrylic, markers collage

Tote
bags.
Neocolos.

↑ *Winehouse* and *Mossy*, portraits of Amy Winehouse and Kate Moss, 2008, personal work (from "50 Bucks: Bring On The Sluts" series); mixed media on paper, pens, gouache, acrylic, markers, collage

→→ *Pammy*, portrait of Pamela Anderson, 2008, personal work (from "50 Bucks: Bring On The Sluts" series); mixed media on paper, pens, gouache, acrylic, markers, collage

PAMMY

Montse Bernal

lives and works in Turin, Italy
www.montsebernal.com

AGENT
Kate Larkworthy Artist
Representation
www.larkworthy.com

"Portraits allow me to rediscover a person. Drawing someone goes beyond the surface of what is shown to us at first glance and what can be touched."

„Mit Porträts kann ich eine Person neu entdecken. Beim Porträtieren einer Person gelangen wir unter die Oberfläche dessen, was uns auf den ersten Blick gezeigt wird und was berührt werden kann."

« Les portraits me permettent de redécouvrir une personne. En dessinant quelqu'un, on va au-delà de la surface de ce qui apparaît au premier regard et de ce qui peut être touché. »

↑   Cordula Daus, 2008, *One Hundred Portraits, Two birds and One Love Song*, book; pen and graphite

→   *Elena*, 2008, *One Hundred Portraits, Two birds and One Love Song*, book; colour pencils, embroidery

→→ Gwyneth Paltrow, 2008, *One Hundred Portraits, Two birds and One Love Song*, book; colour pencils, collage

PICASSO
EN
PRIVAT

↑   *Olga*, 2009, *Embroidering and Whispering*, book; colour pencils, graphite, embroidery on vintage paper

→   Josephine Bonaparte, 2009, *Embroidering and Whispering*, book; colour pencils, graphite, embroidery on vintage paper

←←   Lee Miller, 2008, *One Hundred Portraits, Two birds and One Love Song*, book; colour pencils, embroidery

←← Frida Kahlo, 2008, *One Hundred Portraits, Two birds and One Love Song*, book; colour pencils, embroidery

→ Jessica Mitford, 2008, *One Hundred Portraits, Two birds and One Love Song*, book; colour pencils

↓ *Clarice*, 2008, *One Hundred Portraits, Two birds and One Love Song*, book; colour pencils, graphite

Eduardo Bertone

lives and works in Madrid, Spain
www.bertoneeduardo.com

AGENT
Anna Goodson
Management
www.agoodson.com

> *"Different media get fused in spontaneous, chaotic, and strident ways to wake us up from a sedated and superficial world."*

> *„Unterschiedliche Medien verschmelzen auf spontane, chaotische und schrille Weise, um uns aus einer betäubten und oberflächlichen Welt zu erwecken."*

> *« Différentes techniques fusionnent de façons spontanées, chaotiques et stridentes pour nous réveiller de notre monde apathique et superficiel. »*

↑   *Fifty*, 2010, Anna Goodson Management, promotional; hand drawing, collage, Adobe Photoshop

→   *Amos Showtime*, portrait of Amos, German-Iranian musician, 2010, Amos, *Showtime*, Sounds of Subterrania; collage; in collaboration with Roji

→→ *IdN 15th Anniversary Book* (Hong Kong-Australia), 2009, *IdN*, magazine article; hand drawing, collage, Adobe Photoshop

↑   Portrait of unknown, 2008,
personal work; mixed media on canvas

→→ Portrait of unknown, 2009,
personal work; mixed media on canvas

Annabel Briens

lives and works in Paris, France
www.annabelbriens.com

AGENT
VO Valérie Oualid
France
www.valerieoualid.com

"I often portray people who do not exist, and I like it when people find their friends or their lovers in them."

„Ich porträtiere oft Menschen, die nicht existieren, und mir gefällt es, wenn die Leute ihre Freunde oder Geliebten darin entdecken."

« Je fais souvent des personnes qui n'existent pas, et j'aime bien quand les gens y voient leur amie ou leur amant. »

↑   Samuel Benchetrit, 2010, proposition for Editions Grasset; mixed media, acrylic, oil

→   Portrait of unknown, 2010, *Nico* magazine; mixed media, acrylic, oil

→→ *Bahhh*, 2008, personal work; mixed media, acrylic

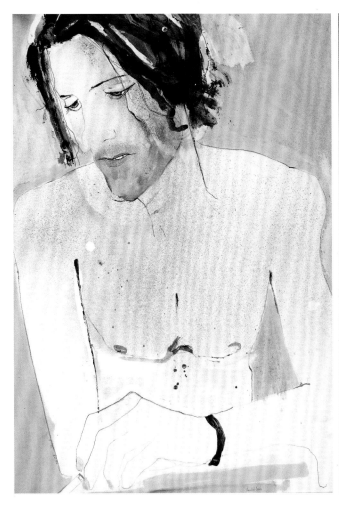

↑   *David*, 2009, personal work;
mixed media, acrylic, oil

→   Frédéric Beigbeder, 2010,
proposition for Editions Grasset,
mixed media, acrylic, oil

←← *Deux filles et tigre*, 2009, personal
work; mixed media, acrylic, oil

↑   *Vernis*, 2009, 2agenten, *Purple*,
book; mixed media, acrylic, oil

→→ *La Diva aux longs cils*, 2010,
Editions Grasset, book cover series;
mixed media, acrylic, oil

Daniel Bueno

lives and works in São Paulo, Brazil
www.buenozine.com.br

*"I work with geometric shapes and collage, asking
the graphic elements to have another meaning.
I like to use abstraction, illusion, and fantasy."*

*„Ich arbeite mit geometrischen Formen und Collagen und bringe
die grafischen Elemente dazu, andere Bedeutungen anzunehmen.
Ich setze gerne Abstraktion, Illusion und Fantasie ein."*

*« Je travaille avec des formes géométriques et des collages, et je
demande aux éléments graphiques de revêtir d'autres significations.
J'aime utiliser l'abstraction, l'illusion et l'imagination. »*

↑ Charles Darwin, 2008, *Ciência Hoje
das Crianças*, magazine article; collage,
Adobe Photoshop

→→ *Loucura na Literatura*, portrait of
the characters: Don Quixote, Woyzeck,
Macbeth, Simão Bacamarte and Bartleby,
2008, *Revista da Cultura*, magazine article;
collage, Adobe Photoshop

↑ Sócrates and Zico 2010, *Football Heroes Gold*, Jerzovskaja, Beach, book; collage and Adobe Photoshop

← Brazil National Football Team 1982, 2006, *Football Heroes*, Ashi & Jerzovskaja, book; collage and Adobe Photoshop

Mike Byers

lives and works in Guelph (ON), Canada
www.michaelbyers.ca

AGENT
Levy Creative Management
www.levycreative.com

> *"I try to capture the essence of who the person is, could be, or as I see them rather than a perfect likeness. It's more fun creating them like that."*
>
> *„Ich versuche, die Essenz dessen einzufangen, wer die Person ist oder sein könnte oder wie ich sie sehe – anstatt es auf eine perfekte Ähnlichkeit anzulegen. Es macht viel mehr Spaß, sie auf diese Weise zu schaffen."*
>
> *« J'essaie de saisir l'essence de ce que la personne est ou pourrait être, ou de ma façon de la voir, plutôt que de la représenter avec une parfaite fidélité. C'est plus intéressant de les créer comme ça. »*

↑   *Hollywood in Hawaii*, 2010,
Honolulu magazine, editorial; ink, digital

→   Mike Byers, self-portrait, 2009,
Uppercase Gallery, *Work/Life* book;
ink, digital

→→ *I've Done It Again*, portrait of Chad
Smith, Red Hot Chili Peppers, 2009,
Bepo + Mimi, gallery show; ink, digital

↑   *Everyone's A Critic*, portrait of
Craig Claiborne, 2010, *Columbia
Journalism Review*, editorial; ink, digital

←←   *LAND*, portrait of Rob Nicholls
aka Land, 2010, poster; ink, digital

↑   *The Humans Are Dead*, portrait
of Flight of the Conchords, 2008,
personal work, poster; ink, digital

→→ *Singing My Guts Out*, 2010, personal
work, promotional; ink, digital

André Carrilho

lives and works in Lisbon, Portugal
www.andrecarrilho.com

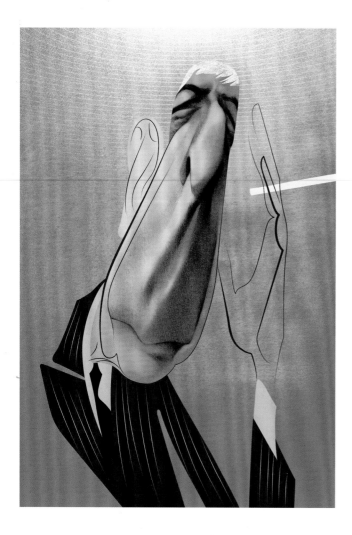

*"When drawing a portrait I try
to pick up on the psychological as
well as the physical characteristics
of the person in question."*

*„Wenn ich ein Porträt male, versuche ich,
sowohl die psychologischen Eigenarten
als auch die körperlichen Kennzeichen
der jeweiligen Person aufzugreifen."*

*« Lorsque je dessine un portrait, j'essaie
de saisir les caractéristiques psychologiques
et physiques de la personne en question. »*

↑ Leonard Cohen, 2008,
The Independent; graphite
on paper, Adobe Photoshop

→ *Heroes & Villains series*, portrait
of Pete Seeger, 2009, *The Independent*;
graphite on paper, Adobe Photoshop

→→ Antonio Lobo Antunes, 2009,
The New Yorker; graphite on paper,
Adobe Photoshop

← Dizzy Gillespie and Frank Zappa, 2010, *Word* magazine; graphite on paper, Adobe Photoshop

→→ Hedy Lamarr, 2005, *The Independent*; graphite on paper, Adobe Photoshop

↑   Wolfgang Amadeus Mozart, 2006,
Diário de Notícias; graphite on paper,
Adobe Photoshop

←← Sigmund Freud, 2007, *RTP*;
graphite on paper, Adobe Photoshop

Lesja Chernish

lives and works in Berlin, Germany
www.i-delicious.de

AGENT

2agenten
Berlin
www.2agenten.com

Bang! Bang! Studio
Moscow
www.bangbangstudio.ru

Private View Illustration
UK
www.pvuk.com

*"Everyone wears a charm
in the face: some like it."*

*„Jeder Mensch trägt einen Zauber
im Gesicht: Irgendeinem gefällt er."*

*« Tout le monde porte un charme
dans le visage : il plaît à certains. »*

— Friedrich Hebbel

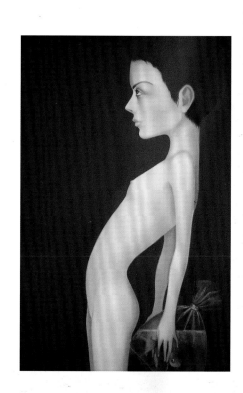

↑ *Birds*, portrait of Miranda Smith, 2010, personal
work, exhibition; acrylic on canvas

→ *Good catch*, portrait of Kim, 2010, personal work,
exhibition; acrylic on canvas

→→ *Café Donath*, portrait of Salomé, 2010, personal
work, exhibition; acrylic on canvas

↑   *Sisters*, portrait of Lula Rubinstein and
Lala Rubinstein, 2010, personal work, exhibition;
acrylic on canvas

→→ Lesja Chernish, self-portrait, 2010,
personal work, exhibition; acrylic on canvas

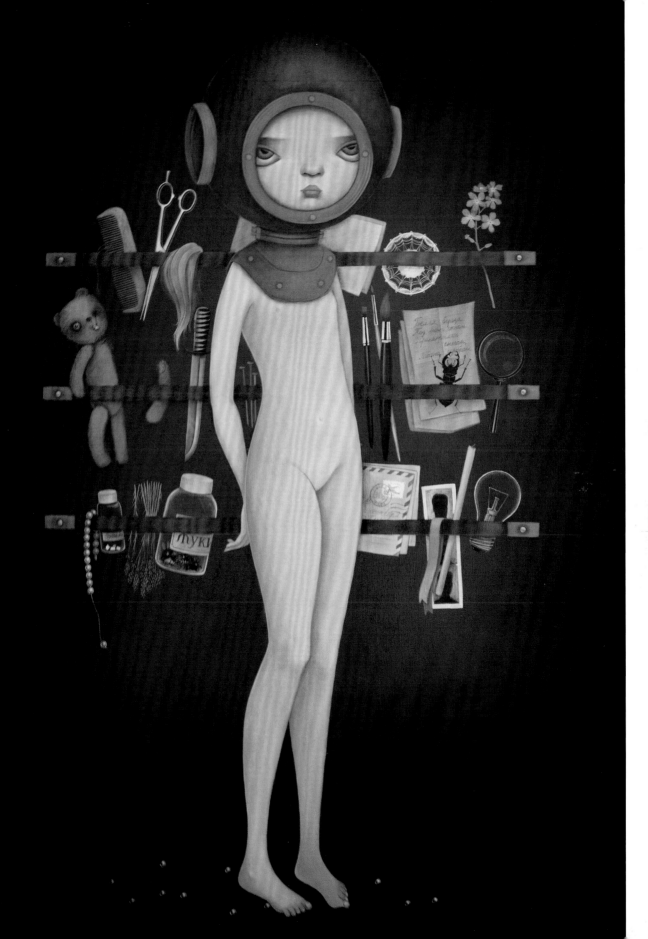

Marcos Chin

lives and works in Brooklyn (NY), USA
www.marcoschin.com

"*I like to include concepts within my portraits that help describe the type of person who I am drawing in order to make the piece more intriguing.*"

„*Ich nehme in meine Porträts gerne Konzepte auf, die dabei helfen, den Typ der Person zu beschreiben, die ich male, um das Werk noch fesselnder zu gestalten.*"

«*J'aime incorporer à mes portraits des concepts qui aident à décrire le type de personne que je dessine afin de rendre le résultat plus intéressant.*»

↑   Jack Johnson, 2008, *Rolling Stone* magazine; ink, Adobe Illustrator, Adobe Photoshop

→→ *A Family Portrait*, portrait of Michael Jackson, 2005, *Spin* magazine; ink, Adobe Illustrator, Adobe Photoshop

↑   The Beatles, 2009, *Paste* magazine;
ink, Adobe Illustrator, Adobe Photoshop

←← Beyoncé, 2006, *Vibe* magazine;
Adobe Illustrator, Adobe Photoshop

Joe Ciardiello

lives and works in Milford (NJ), USA
www.joeciardiello.com

↑   Antonio Meucci, 2006,
personal work; pen, ink, watercolour

→   Edgar Allan Poe, 2005,
personal work; pen, ink

→→ Mark Twain, 2009, *Humanities*,
magazine article; pen, ink, watercolour

Les Paul

←← Lester William Polsfuss aka Les Paul, 2010,
personal work; pen, ink, watercolour

→   Clint Eastwood, 2005, personal work; pen, ink

↘   John Updike, 2007, *The New York Times*,
newspaper article; pen, ink

↓   David Mamet, 2007, *The New York Times*,
newspaper article; pen, ink

Sarah Cline

lives and works in Croton-On-Hudson (NY), USA

AGENT
Kate Larkworthy Artist
Representation
www.larkworthy.com

"I really enjoy working on portraits. I like to focus on the precision and details of the facial features while patterns emerge in the background."

„Ich arbeite ausgesprochen gerne an Porträts. Mir gefällt es, mich auf die Präzision und Details der Gesichtszüge zu konzentrieren, während im Hintergrund die Muster entstehen."

«J'aime vraiment beaucoup travailler sur les portraits. J'aime me concentrer sur la précision et les détails des traits du visage tandis que des motifs émergent à l'arrière-plan.»

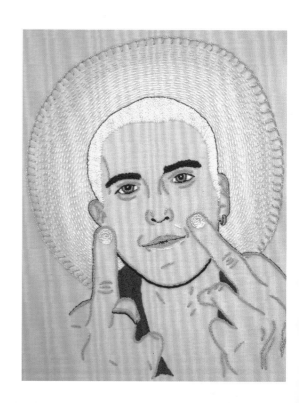

↑   Johnny Depp, 2003, *Flaunt* magazine; embroidery, satin, thread

→   Eminem, 2002, *Flaunt* magazine; embroidery, cotton fabric, thread

→→ *Lux and Morel*, portrait of Lux, my daughter, 2010, personal work; embroidery, cotton fabric, thread

Tavis Coburn

lives and works in Toronto, Canada
www.taviscoburn.com

"When I'm working on a portrait, I try to focus on creating a sense of drama and movement."

„Wenn ich an einem Porträt arbeite, konzentriere ich mich darauf, den Eindruck von Dramatik und Bewegung zu vermitteln."

« Lorsque je travaille sur un portrait, j'essaie de créer une impression théâtrale, et de mouvement. »

↑   Martin Luther King Jr., 2008, *Atlanta* magazine, editorial; Maxon Cinema 4D, Corel Painter, Adobe Creative Suite

→   Gabourey Sidibe, 2010, British Academy of Film & Television Arts, award show programme cover; Maxon Cinema 4D, Corel Painter, Adobe Creative Suite

→→ Steven Tyler, 2005, *Boston* magazine, editorial; Maxon Cinema 4D, Corel Painter, Adobe Creative Suite

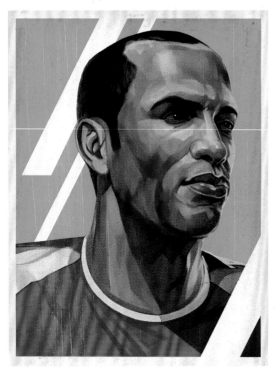

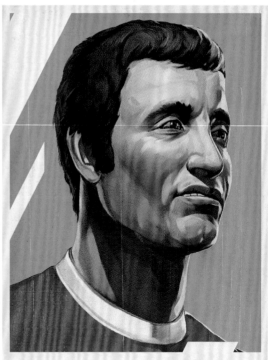

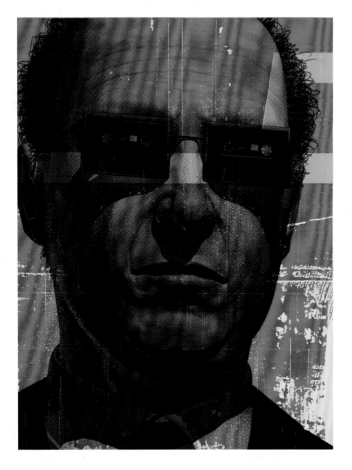

↑ Thierry Henry and Frank McLintock, 2010, Arsenal F.C., portrait for Emirates Stadium; Maxon Cinema 4D, Corel Painter, Adobe Creative Suite

← Anthony Pellicano, 2007, *Los Angeles* magazine, editorial opener; Maxon Cinema 4D, Corel Painter, Adobe Creative Suite

→→ Sam Worthington as Jake Sully in the movie *Avatar*, 2010, British Academy of Film & Television Arts, award show programme cover; Maxon Cinema 4D, Corel Painter, Adobe Creative Suite

Alexandra Compain-Tissier

lives and works in Paris, France
www.alexandracompaintissier.com

AGENT
Art Department
www.art-dept.com

"I believe in the magic of the painting so when I do a portrait I can feel close to the model even if I don't know him."

„Ich glaube an die Magie des Malens. Wenn ich also an einem Porträt arbeite, fühle ich mich dem Modell sehr nahe, auch wenn ich es nicht weiter kenne."

« Je crois à la magie de la peinture, alors quand je fais un portrait je peux me sentir proche du modèle même si je ne le connais pas. »

↑   Michel Blanc, 2008, *GQ France*, magazine article; watercolour on paper

→   Sophie Toporkoff, 2006, *BPM*, France, magazine article; pencil and watercolour on paper

→→ Matthew Barney, 2004, *Agenda*, France, magazine article; pencil and watercolour on paper

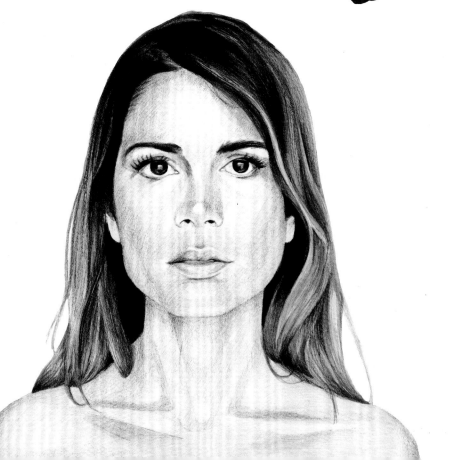

↑   Helene Gayle, 2009,
Atlanta magazine, article;
watercolour on paper

↗   Frank Kozik, 2009,
Wired magazine, article;
watercolour on paper

→   *Eté d'amour*, Alexandra
Compain-Tissier, self-portrait,
2005, *Respect in Burning*,
poster and flyer; pencil and
watercolour on paper

←← Suri Cruise, 2010,
Gala, Germany, magazine
article; watercolour on paper

→ *The Cowboy*, portrait of Pascal Jalabert, 2007, *Blast*, France, magazine article; pencil on paper

↓ Ruslan Karablin aka SSUR, 2004, *The Source* magazine, fashion story; pencil on paper

→→ *Infernal Affairs actors*, 2004, All Rights Reserved Ltda., Hong Kong, DVD cover; pencil on paper

Augusto Costanzo

lives and works in Buenos Aires, Argentina
www.costhanzo.com

"I always try to achieve a marriage between a good synthesis of the character and its image, and a solid idea, no matter how simple it is."

„*Ich versuche immer, die gute Darstellung des Charakters sowie dessen Abbild mit einer soliden Idee zu verheiraten – egal wie schlicht die Idee ist.*"

«*J'essaie toujours d'arriver à un mariage entre une bonne synthèse du personnage et de son image, et une idée solide, même si elle est très simple.*»

↑   *Andy Warhol & Campbell's Soup*, portrait of Andy Warhol, 2007, *Alma* magazine, article; Adobe Illustrator

→   *Hero & Villain*, portrait of John McCririck, 2010, *The Independent*, newspaper article; Adobe Illustrator

→→ *School of Fidelity*, portrait of Jack Black, 2009, personal work, exhibition; Adobe Illustrator

↑ *La Liberté*, portrait of Sophia Loren, 2008, personal work; Adobe Illustrator

←← *World Cup 2010*, portraits of Lionel Messi, Cristiano Ronaldo, Diego Forlan, Gianluigi Buffon, Wayne Rooney and Kaka, 2010, *Marca*, Spain, newspaper article; Adobe Illustrator

Jean-Philippe Delhomme

lives and works in New York (NY), USA
www.jphdelhomme.com

AGENT
Jed Root Inc.
www.jedroot.com

*"Expressing someone's personality
with the fewest, but essential details.
Always suggesting the body
language and physical presence,
not just the face."*

*„Die Persönlichkeit sollte nur mit den wenigsten, aber
wesentlichsten Details ausgedrückt werden. Nicht nur
das Gesicht, sondern auch die Körpersprache und
die physische Präsenz sollten spürbar sein."*

*« Exprimer la personnalité de quelqu'un avec le moins
de détails possible, mais des détails essentiels.
Toujours suggérer le langage du corps et la présence
physique, pas seulement le visage. »*

↑ Iggy Pop, 2009, *La Tribune*,
magazine article; gouache

→ Michelle Obama, 2009, BBH,
book; gouache

→→ Karl Lagerfeld, 2009, *Whitewall*
magazine, cover; gouache

↑   Hamish Bowles, 2010, New York
City Opera Thrift Shop, invitation card;
colour pencil

→   Terry Richardson, 2009, personal
work, exhibition; colour pencil

←← *Damien Hirst at Gagosian*, portrait
of Damien Hirst, 2010, personal work,
blog; gouache

↑ Vivienne Westwood, 2010, *Muse*,
magazine article; gouache

→ Kate Moss, 2010, *Milk X* magazine,
magazine article; gouache

→→ Marcel Wanders, 2010, *Schöner
Wohnen*, magazine article; gouache

Vanessa Dell

lives and works in Surrey, UK
www.vanessadell.com

"I like to capture a face at its most vulnerable, with all the interesting imperfections. No gloss, no fluff, the raw basics with a depth of character."

„Mir gefällt es, ein Gesicht möglichst verletzlich zu zeigen, mit allen interessanten Unzulänglichkeiten. Kein Glanz, kein Aufhübschen, nur die Basics und die Tiefe des Charakters."

« J'aime saisir un visage dans son état le plus vulnérable, avec toutes ses imperfections fascinantes. Pas de glamour, pas de coquetteries, juste les bases brutes avec une profondeur de caractère. »

↑　*Alan Partridge et al.*, portrait of Alan Partridge with some of Steve Coogan's other characters, 2007, *The New Yorker*, magazine article; hand painting, oil on treated paper

→　*Young Prince Charles*, portrait of Prince Charles, 2008, *Annabelle*, Switzerland, magazine article; hand painting, oil on treated paper

→→ Audrey Hepburn, 2008, *Annabelle*, Switzerland, magazine article; hand painting, oil on treated paper

→→ Thom Yorke, Amy Winehouse and Alexis Taylor, 2008, *Musikexpress* magazine, Germany, cover; hand painting, oil on treated paper

← Milos Forman, film director, 2006, *Annabelle*, Switzerland, magazine article; hand painting, oil on treated paper

↙ *Heroes of Gear*, 2007, *Bicycling and Mountain Bike* magazine, article; hand painting, oil on paper

↓ *Heroes of Gear*, portrait of Joel Smith, bike industry veteran, 2007, *Bicycling and Mountain Bike* magazine, article; hand painting, oil on paper

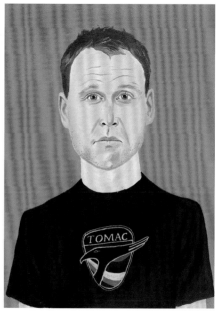

↑   Niklaus Meienberg, 2008, *Annabelle*, Switzerland,
magazine article; hand painting, oil on paper

↑   Alfred Hitchcock and Dr. Frederic Wertham, 2008, *Annabelle*,
Switzerland, magazine article; hand painting, oil on paper

David Despau

lives and works in Madrid, Spain
www.despau.com

"I like to draw faces with the simplest means (pencil, ballpoint pen, ink…) to emphasise a point of interest and then dilute the rest to create a beautiful composition."

„Ich zeichne Gesichter gerne mit einfachsten Mitteln (Bleistift, Kuli, Tinte …), um einen interessanten Aspekt zu betonen. Den Rest schwäche ich dann ab, um eine schöne Komposition zu schaffen."

« J'aime dessiner les visages avec les moyens les plus simples (crayon, stylo, encre …) afin d'accentuer un certain aspect et de diluer le reste pour créer une belle composition. »

↑ David Beckham, 2010, personal work,
poster; hand drawing, ink, ballpoint pen,
Adobe Photoshop

→ Lenny Kravitz, 2009, personal work;
hand drawing, ink, ballpoint pen,
Adobe Photoshop

→→ Rachel Weisz, 2010, personal work;
hand drawing, ink, ballpoint pen,
Adobe Photoshop

↑　*Hair wig*, 2010, personal work; hand drawing, ink, ballpoint pen, Adobe Photoshop

→→　*Mad women*, portrait of Christina Hendricks, 2010, personal work; hand drawing, watercolour, ballpoint pen, Adobe Photoshop

Mark Dickson

lives and works in Sherwood (Nottingham), UK
www.i-am-mark.com

AGENT
Folio
www.folioart.co.uk

"I start out with traditional media and then experiment with layering, texture, and composition; interested in conveying mood as well as likeness."

„Ich beginne mit traditionellen Medien und experimentiere dann mit Schichtung, Texturen und Komposition. Neben einer Ähnlichkeit des Bildes bin ich genauso daran interessiert, Stimmungen zu vermittel."

« Je commence avec des techniques traditionnelles, puis j'expérimente sur la superposition, la texture et la composition ; je veux faire un portrait ressemblant physiquement, mais je veux aussi exprimer une humeur. »

↑   *The River Cottage*, portrait of Hugh Fearnley-Whittingstall, 2009, personal work; pen, ink, watercolour, digital photography, Adobe Photoshop

→   Vivienne Westwood, 2010, personal work; pen, ink, watercolour, spray paint, digital photography, Adobe Photoshop

→→ *River Cottage*, portrait of Ray Smith, 2009, personal work; pen, ink, watercolour, cardboard, Adobe Photoshop

↑   *Continental Philosophers series*,
portraits of Michel Foucault, Jacques
Derrida, Jacques Lacan, 2010, personal
work; pen, ink, watercolour, digital
photography, Adobe Photoshop

←← Queen Elizabeth II, 2010, personal
work; pen, ink, watercolour, digital
photography, Adobe Photoshop

Glauco Diogenes

lives and works in São Paulo, Brazil
www.glaucodiogenes.com.br

"I look with excitement at every character I want to portray. And each one looks back at me to allow me to explore it fully."

„Ich schaue mir mit Spannung jede Person an, die ich porträtieren will. Und jede schaut wiederum mich an und erlaubt mir, sie umfassend zu erforschen."

« Je porte un regard enthousiaste sur chaque personnage dont je veux faire le portrait. Et chacun me rend ce regard pour me permettre de l'explorer pleinement. »

↑　Edison Arantes do Nascimento, "Pelé", 2010, São Paulo Futebol Clube, tickets, magazine, book, football shirts; hand drawing, collage, scanner, vector illustration, Adobe Photoshop

→　Pope John Paul II, 2010, São Paulo Futebol Clube, tickets, magazine, book, football shirts; hand drawing, collage, scanner, vector illustration, Adobe Photoshop

→→ Madonna, 2009, personal work; hand drawing, collage, scanner, vector illustration, Adobe Photoshop

Jan Feindt

lives and works in Berlin, Germany
www.janfeindt.de

AGENT

Gerald & Cullen Rapp
New York
www.rappart.com

pln.management
London
www.plnmanagement.com

*"The pose of the model has to be interesting.
There has to be a lot of expression in the face."*

*„Die Pose des Modells muss interessant sein. Im Gesicht
sollte man möglichst viel Ausdruck finden."*

*« Le modèle doit prendre une pose intéressante.
Il doit avoir un visage très expressif. »*

↑   Stephenie Meyer, 2009,
Der Spiegel, magazine article;
pen, brush, ink, Adobe Photoshop

→→ Vincent Gallo, 2005, personal work;
pen, brush, ink, Adobe Photoshop

↑ TV On The Radio, 2008, *Rolling Stone* magazine, article; pen, brush, ink, Adobe Photoshop

←← Courtney Love, 2007, Illustrative 2007, exhibition; pen, brush, ink, Adobe Photoshop

Owen Freeman

lives and works in Los Angeles (CA), USA
www.owenfreeman.com

AGENT
Heflinreps
www.heflinreps.com

*"I try to approach portrait illustration
as a narrative reflected in a subject."*

*„Ich versuche, die Illustration eines Porträts
wie eine Geschichte anzugehen, die sich
in einem Subjekt niederschlägt."*

*« J'essaie d'aborder le portrait d'illustration comme
une histoire qui se reflète dans un sujet. »*

↑   January Jones, 2010, Heflinreps,
promotional calendar; ink, digital

→→ *Brutal Lemmy*, portrait of
Lemmy Kilmister, 2009, *Nylon Guys*,
magazine article; ink, digital

↑　*Conchords*, portrait of Flight of the Conchords, 2009, personal work; ink, digital

↖　*Lost*, portrait of Matthew Fox, 2010, *The Washington Post*, newspaper article; ink, digital

←←　*Treme*, portrait of Wendell Pierce, 2010, *The Washington Post*, newspaper article; ink, digital

Carmen García Huerta

lives and works in Madrid, Spain
www.cghuerta.com

AGENT

Agent 002
Paris
www.agent002.com

V&W art
Madrid
www.vandwart.com

Clicks and Contacts
London
www.clicksandcontacts.com

"Completely organic. Radically opposite to my neat commercial illustrations. Skin is the real battlefield, with real or invented flaws, almost rotting."

„Völlig organisch. Radikal das Gegenteil zu meinen netten kommerziellen Illustrationen. Die Haut, beinah verwelkt, ist das wahre Schlachtfeld mit echten oder erfundenen Macken."

« Complètement organique. Radicalement opposé à mes illustrations commerciales, très propres. La peau est un vrai champ de bataille, avec des défauts réels ou inventés, presque en décomposition. »

↑   Madonna, 2010, personal
work, exhibition; hand drawing

→   Laura Ponte, 2008,
Arte de Vivir, magazine editorial;
hand drawing

→→ Grace Coddington, 2010,
personal work; hand drawing

↑ Morrissey, 2009, *Buffalo*,
magazine article; hand drawing

←← Eleonora Bosé, 2010, *Moose*,
magazine article; hand drawing

Andreas Gefe

lives and works in Zürich, Switzerland
www.gefe.ch

"I like to tell a story."

„Ich erzähle gerne eine Geschichte."

« J'aime raconter une histoire. »

← *Im Tal*, portrait of Theresa, 2009, personal work, postcard; acrylic

→→ *Lady Snowblood*, portrait of Yuki Kashima, 2007, ETH Filmstelle, Cinema, poster and postcard; acrylic

↓↓ *Herzrasen*, Andreas Gefe, self-portrait with friends, 2008, ASFV, Alternative Swiss Football League, book; acrylic

↑   *Im Schatte vo däm Bärg*, portrait of
Christoph Trummer, 2008, Christoph
Trummer, CD cover and poster; acrylic

←← *Café Einstein*, portrait of Wolfram
Siebeck, 2007, *Playboy* Germany,
magazine article; acrylic

Michael Gillette

lives and works in San Francisco (CA), USA
www.michaelgillette.com

"*Painting portraits is about spending meditative time with the subject whether they are in the room or not.*"

„*Beim Malen von Porträts geht es darum, mit dem Porträtierten eine meditative Zeit zu verbringen, egal ob er sich im Raum befindet oder nicht.*"

« *Peindre des portraits signifie de passer un moment méditatif avec le sujet, que le sujet soit là ou pas.* »

↑   *The Ballad of John & Yoko*, portrait of John Lennon and Yoko Ono, 2006, personal work; pencil

→   Elliott Smith, 2009, Chronicle Books, book cover; pen, ink, digital coloured

→→ Beck, 2006, watercolour

↑　Michael Cera, 2010, *Little White Lies*
magazine, *Scott Pilgrim vs. the World*
promotional; watercolour

→　Bob Dylan, 2009, Chronicle Books,
book; pen, ink, digital coloured

→→　*An education*, portrait of Carey
Mulligan, 2009, *Little White Lies*
magazine; chalk on chalkboard

Good Wives and Warriors

live and work in London, UK
www.goodwivesandwarriors.co.uk

AGENT
Central Illustration Agency
London
www.centralillustration.com

The Jacky Winter Group
Melbourne
www.jackywinter.com

"We give anonymous 'spam-senders' faces and identities using Google Image searches. Portraiture allows these Internet pests to be viewed differently."

„Über die Bildsuche von Google verleihen wir den anonymen Versendern von Spam Gesichter und Identitäten. Durch die Porträtmalerei können diese Plagegeister des Internets anders betrachtet werden."

« Nous donnons des visages et des identités aux spammeurs anonymes à l'aide de recherches dans Google Image. Le portrait permet de voir différemment cette espèce nuisible qui sévit sur Internet. »

↑　*Hymen Destroyer*, portrait of Lorie Winkler, 2010, Spam Senders, Volume 8; pen and pencil on paper

→　*Gigantic Meat Poles in Action for $1*, portrait of Bryce Bravo, 2010, Spam Senders, Volume 6; pen and pencil on paper

→→ *Plysexual Bad Taste Fondue Party*, portrait of Karen Valentine, 2010, Spam Senders, Volume 7; pen and pencil on paper

← ← *Your little love soldier will grow up to be a big love general*, portrait of Major Leach, 2008, Spam Senders, Volume 3; pen on paper

→ *When it absolutely, positively has to be rock hard*, portrait of Noelle Driver, 2008, Spam Senders, Volume 4; pen on paper

↘ *Unleash your trouser mouse*, portrait of Duke Dundee, 2008, Spam Senders, Volume 2; pen on paper

↓ *Pop it twice a day for a bigger sway*, portrait of Trudy Lou, 2008, Spam Senders, Volume 5; pen on paper

Lisa Grue

lives and works in Copenhagen, Denmark
www.underwerket.dk

AGENT
CWC International
www.cwc-i.com

*"We are all so alike
and yet so very different,
that is the beauty of it all."*

*„Wir ähneln einander alle so sehr
und sind doch so verschieden –
das ist das Schöne daran."*

*« Nous sommes tous si semblables
et pourtant si différents,
c'est cela qui est beau. »*

↑ *Patternworld*, 2006, personal work;
watercolour, pencil

→→ *Nylon Girls*, 2007, personal work;
watercolour, crayon

Olaf Hajek

lives and works in Berlin, Germany
www.olafhajek.com

AGENT

2agenten	Bernstein & Andriulli	Pocko
Berlin	New York	London
www.2agenten.com	www.ba-reps.com	www.pocko.com

"The challenge is to create in addition to the Likeness an idea about the vibes and aura of the person I have to portray."

„Die Herausforderung besteht für mich darin, neben der Ähnlichkeit eine Ahnung über Ausstrahlung und Aura der von mir porträtierten Person zu vermitteln."

« Le plus difficile, c'est de créer, en plus de la ressemblance physique, une idée sur les vibrations et l'aura de la personne dont je dois faire le portrait. »

↑   Eddie Mabo, 2009, *Time* magazine, article; acrylic on wood

→   *Shakespeare in the park*, portrait of William Shakespeare, 2008, *San Francisco Chronicle*, newspaper article; acrylic on cardboard

→→ Michelle Obama, 2009, personal work; acrylic on wood

↑   *Charlie Haden and the Sophisticated Ladies*, portrait of Charlie Haden with
Norah Jones, Renée Fleming, Ruth Cameron, Melody Gardot, Diana Krall and
Cassandra Wilson, 2010, Universal Music, Germany; acrylic on cardboard,
press release of Charlie Hadens' album *Sophisticated Ladies*

←← José Mourinho, 2010, *JFK* magazine, Amsterdam, article; acrylic on wood

→→ *Flowerhead*, portrait of Iris Strubegger, 2010, personal work, exhibition Flowerhead; acrylic on paper

← *Black power*, portrait of Malcolm X and Martin Luther King, 2009, Schwarzkopf/ Henkel, series Revolutionary Hair, book *We love hair*, 111 year of Schwarzkopf; acrylic on cardboard

↙ *Whiteblack*, portrait of Shaun Ross, 2010, personal work, exhibition Flowerhead; acrylic on wood

↓ Marie Antoinette, 2009, Schwarzkopf/ Henkel, series Revolutionary Hair, book *We love hair*, 111 year of Schwarzkopf; acrylic on cardboard

Tomer Hanuka

lives and works in New York (NY), USA
www.thanuka.com

*"Illustration is the art
of scene as metaphor."*

„*Illustration ist die szenische
Kunst als Metapher.*"

«*L'illustration, c'est l'art de
la scène comme métaphore.*»

← *Spaced out*, portrait of MGMT, 2010,
Rolling Stone magazine; ink, digital

→→ *In the Garden of Armageddon*,
portrait of Dr. Mahdi Obeidi, 2005,
Mother Jones magazine, cover; ink, digital

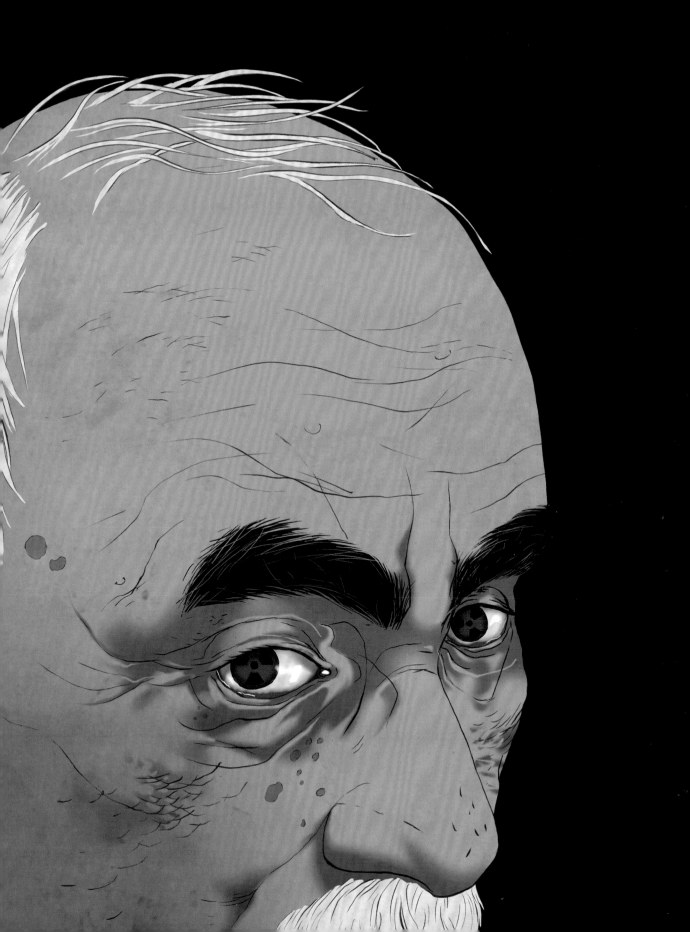

← *The Raging Bull*, portrait of Robert de Niro, 2005, *Entertainment Weekly*, cover; ink, digital

↓ The White Stripes, 2007, *Spin* magazine; ink, digital

↑ *Kill Bill*, portrait of Uma Thurman, 2004, *New York* magazine, ink, digital

↑　*American Gangster*, portrait
of Jay-Z, 2007, *Rolling Stone*
magazine; ink, digital

→→ The Wu-Tang Clan, 2001,
Rolling Stone magazine; ink, digital

Jens Harder

lives and works in Berlin, Germany
www.hardercomics.de

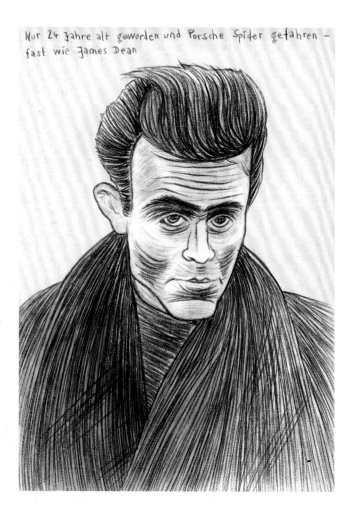

Nur 24 Jahre alt geworden und Porsche Spider gefahren – fast wie James Dean

↑   *Nur 24 Jahre ...*, portrait of a James Dean lookalike, 2006, personal work; hand drawing with coloured pens on paper

→   *Eiserne Lady*, portrait of Margaret Thatcher, 2006, personal work; hand drawing with coloured pens on paper

→→ *Sakamot*, portrait of Ryuichi Sakamoto, 2006, personal work; hand drawing with coloured pens on paper

Jody Hewgill

lives and works in Toronto (ON), Canada
www.jodyhewgill.com

"My portraits are not based on realism but they do reveal some truth. When I paint someone's portrait I feel like I'm having a dialogue with the subject."

„Meine Porträts basieren nicht auf Realismus, aber enthüllen doch eine gewisse Wahrheit. Wenn ich ein Porträt male, fühle ich mich, als befände ich mich in einem Zwiegespräch mit dem Dargestellten."

« Mes portraits ne sont pas basés sur le réalisme, mais ils révèlent une certaine vérité. Lorsque je peins le portrait de quelqu'un, j'ai l'impression d'avoir un dialogue avec le sujet. »

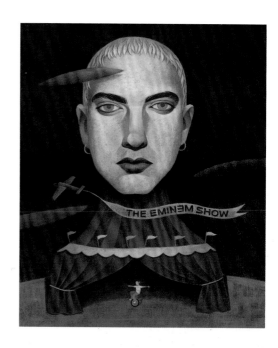

↑   P. J. Harvey, 2001, *Rolling Stone* magazine, article; acrylic on rag board

→   *The Eminem Show*, portrait of Eminem, 2002, *Vibe*, magazine article; acrylic on rag board

→→   *The Sopranos*, portrait of James Gandolfini and Annabella Sciorra, 2001, *Entertainment Weekly*, magazine article; acrylic on rag board

↑   *The Roman Spring of Mr. Morrissey*,
portrait of Morrissey, 2006, *Spin* magazine,
article; acrylic on rag board

→   Rihanna, 2009, *Rolling Stone* magazine,
article; acrylic on rag board

↑ *Death of an Addict*, portrait of
Michael Jackson, 2009, *Los Angeles*
magazine, article; acrylic on rag board

→→ *Hey, I lost my head*, portrait of Kirsten Dunst, 2006, *Los Angeles* magazine, article; acrylic on rag board

↓ *Jury Diddy*, portrait of P. Diddy, 2001, *Entertainment Weekly*, magazine article; acrylic on rag board

↑ *Putin's New Evil Empire*, portrait of Vladimir Putin, 2008, *Standpoint* magazine, article; acrylic on rag board

→ Kanye West, 2008, *Rolling Stone* magazine, article; acrylic on rag board

Tiago Hoisel

lives and works in Salvador (Bahia), Brazil
http://hoisel.zip.net

"*I try to make my portraits with a funnier and more humorous interpretation of people. Sometimes I end up transforming them into cartoon characters.*"

„*Ich versuche, meine Porträts mit einer eher lustigen und humorvollen Interpretation der Menschen zu schaffen. Manchmal verwandele ich sie am Ende in Zeichentrickcharaktere.*"

«*J'essaie de faire en sorte que mes portraits donnent une interprétation des gens plus drôle, plus humoristique. Parfois, je finis par les transformer en personnages de dessins animés.*»

↑   Hugh Jackman as Wolverine, 2008, personal work; Adobe Photoshop

→   *Pelé, the King*, portrait of Edison Arantes do Nascimento, "Pelé", 2009, personal work; Adobe Photoshop

→→ *Stallone-Rambo*, portrait of Sylvester Stallone, 2008, personal work; Adobe Photoshop

Josie Jammet

lives and works in London, UK

AGENT
Heart
www.heartagency.com

"*There is plenty of subjectivity in the process of painting a portrait; even if it is mostly at a subconscious level.*"

„*Im Prozess der Porträtmalerei gibt es sehr viel Subjektivität, auch wenn sich das meistens auf einer unterbewussten Ebene abspielt.*"

« *Il y a beaucoup de subjectivité dans la peinture de portrait ; même si elle se situe surtout au niveau de l'inconscient.* »

↑   Angela Carter, 2005, *Guardian Review* magazine; acrylic on canvas

→   Tom Cruise as Colonel Claus von Stauffenberg in the movie *Valkyrie*, 2009, *Esquire* magazine; acrylic on canvas

→→ Stanley Kubrick, 2009, *Sight and Sound* magazine; acrylic on canvas

↑ *The Queen's Sister*, portrait of
Lucy Cohu, actress, 2006, Channel 4
Annual Report; acrylic on canvas

←← Jamie Oliver, 2006, Channel 4
Annual Report; acrylic on canvas

Aaron Jasinski

lives and works in Seattle (WA), USA
www.aaronjasinski.com

*"My approach is to capture something of the subject's personality
and spirit through color and unconventional environments."*

*„In meinem Ansatz versuche ich, durch Farbe und eine unkonventionelle Umgebung
etwas von der Persönlichkeit und dem Geist des Porträtierten einzufangen."*

*« Mon approche consiste à saisir quelque chose de la personnalité
et de l'esprit du sujet à travers la couleur et des décors originaux. »*

↑ *Rush*, portrait of Geoffrey
Rush, 2005, personal work; digital

→→ *Let Love In*, portrait of Mae West,
2009, Gallery 1988, gallery
exhibition; acrylic

↑ *Brass vs. Funky*, portrait of Beastie Boys, 2008,
Gallery 1988, themed group exhibition; acrylic

→ Lauren Bacall, 2005, personal work; digital

→→ Angelina Jolie, 2005, personal work; digital

↑ *Gathering the Troops*, portrait of Marlene Dietrich,
2009, Gallery 1988, gallery exhibition; acrylic

Jules Julien

lives and works in Paris, France
www.julesjulien.com

AGENT

VO Valérie Oualid
France
www.valerieoualid.com

Hugo & Marie
New York
www.hugoandmarie.com

MW Company
Tokyo and Shanghai
www.mw-company.com

"Playing with the reality of the subject and unreality of the drawing."

„Ein Spiel mit der Realität des Subjekts und der Irrealität der Zeichnung."

« Jouer avec la réalité du sujet et l'irréalité du dessin. »

↑   Michael Ferguson, 2010, *PaperJam*,
magazine supplement; Adobe Illustrator

→   Theresa Hamacher, 2010, *PaperJam*,
magazine supplement; Adobe Illustrator

→→ *Jouissance*, portrait of Roger, 2008,
PREF, magazine article; Adobe Illustrator,
with the collaboration of Brett Lloyd

Kako

lives and works in São Paulo, Brazil
www.kakofonia.com

AGENT
Levy Creative Management
www.levycreative.com

*"No matter how good you are, you're always
a nose away from a caricature."*

*„Egal wie gut du bist, von einer Karikatur bist du immer
nur eine Nasenlänge entfernt."*

*« Aussi talentueux que l'on puisse être, on est toujours
à un nez de distance de la caricature. »*

↑   *The Future of Record Labels*, portrait
of Mauro Motoki, 2007, Editora Abril,
magazine article; Adobe Illustrator,
Adobe Photoshop

→→ *Red Planet*, portrait of Mao Tse-Tung,
Joseph Stalin, Vladimir Lenin, Hugo
Chávez and Ernesto "Che" Guevara, 2007,
Editora Globo, magazine article;
Adobe Illustrator, Adobe Photoshop

→→ *Connection 1969*, portrait of
Anderson Noise, 2008, DVD cover;
Adobe Illustrator, Adobe Photoshop

↓ *.bug*, portrait of Marty Feldman,
2006, *Revista Colectiva*, Insects Edition,
magazine article; Adobe Illustrator,
Adobe Photoshop

↓   Os Mutantes: Rita Lee, Arnaldo
Baptista and Sérgio Dias Baptista,
2006, personal work; Adobe Illustrator,
Adobe Photoshop

Christopher Kasch

lives and works in Harrow (Middlesex), UK
www.chriskasch.co.uk

AGENT

Central Illustration
Agency, London
www.centralillustration.com

B+A
New York
www.ba-reps.com

"Capture the essence of the person you are painting, if you need a caption below the image to inform the viewer who it is then you have failed."

„Fang die Essenz der Person ein, die du malst. Wenn du eine Bildunterschrift brauchst, damit der Betrachter sieht, wer gemeint ist, hast du versagt."

« Capturez l'essence de la personne que vous peignez. S'il vous faut une légende sous l'image pour dire aux gens de qui il s'agit, vous avez échoué. »

↑ Mike Tyson, 2002, *Esquire* magazine; acrylic on paper

→ Elton John, 2002, UTV Music, Universal Music Group; acrylic on paper

→→ Aaron Sorkin, 2006, *New York* magazine; acrylic on paper

↑   Amir Pnueli, 2009, Communications
of the ACM; acrylic on paper

↗   Portrait of unknown, 2007,
Business Week magazine; acrylic on paper

→   Robert Downey Jr., 2001,
Time Out magazine; acrylic on paper

←← Ken Livingstone, 2006,
Estates Gazette; acrylic on paper

←← The Ramones, 2005, *Rolling Stone*
magazine; acrylic on paper

→   Neil Young, 2005, *Q* magazine;
acrylic on paper

↓   Gordon Downie, 2003,
Toro magazine; acrylic on paper

Jörn Kaspuhl

lives and works in Hamburg, Germany
www.kaspuhl.com

AGENT
Dutch Uncle
www.dutchuncle.co.uk

"*I love to portray artists, especially musicians, because music is the biggest influence on my life and my work.*"

„*Ich liebe es, Künstler zu porträtieren, vor allem Musiker, weil Musik auf mein Leben und meine Arbeit den größten Einfluss ausübt.*"

«*J'aime faire des portraits d'artistes, surtout de musiciens, parce que la musique est ma plus grande influence dans la vie et dans le travail.*»

↑   Sufjan Stevens, 2009, *Rolling Stone* magazine; ink, Adobe Photoshop

→   Bat for Lashes, 2009, personal work; ink, Adobe Photoshop

→→ *Yeah Yeah Yeahs*, portrait of Karen O, 2009, *Rolling Stone* magazine; ink, Adobe Photoshop

↑   Sufjan Stevens, 2010, personal work;
ink, Adobe Photoshop

←   Antony and the Johnsons, 2010,
Rolling Stone magazine;
ink, Adobe Photoshop

→ Coco Rosie, 2008, personal work;
ink, Adobe Photoshop

↓ David Bowie, 2008, personal work;
ink, Adobe Photoshop

Ben Kirchner

lives and works in Bath, UK
www.benkirchner.co.uk

AGENT
Heart
www.heartagency.com

"I like to create portraits that somehow feel more like the subject than a photo would. I think this is a good thing to aim for when creating portraits."

„Ich schaffe gerne Porträts, die mehr von der dargestellten Person vermitteln, als ein Foto das könnte. Das ist meiner Meinung nach erstrebenswert, wenn man Porträts schafft."

« J'aime créer des portraits qui d'une certaine manière ressemblent plus au sujet qu'une photo. Je pense que c'est un bon objectif à avoir lorsqu'on fait des portraits. »

↑   Russel Crowe, 2009, *The Guardian*, weekly column "A peek at the diary" by Marina Hyde; Adobe Illustrator, Adobe Photoshop

→   Courtney Love, 2007, *The Guardian*, weekly column "A peek at the diary" by Marina Hyde; Adobe Illustrator

→→ Pete Doherty, 2007, personal work; Adobe Illustrator

↑   Vincent Gallo, 2007,
personal work; Adobe Illustrator

→   Danger Mouse, 2007,
personal work; Adobe Illustrator

←← John C. Reilly, 2007,
personal work; Adobe Illustrator

↑ Nicolas Cage, Bono Vox, Kevin Pietersen, 2009,
The Guardian, weekly column "A peek at the diary"
by Marina Hyde; Adobe Illustrator, Adobe Photoshop

→→ Barack Obama, 2008, *The New Republic*, book;
Adobe Illustrator, Adobe Photoshop

↓ Brad Pitt, 2008, *The Guardian*, weekly
column "A peek at the diary" by Marina Hyde;
Adobe Illustrator, Adobe Photoshop

Ilana Kohn

lives and works in Brooklyn (NY), USA
www.ilanakohn.com

← Robert Jamieson,
Seattle columnist, 2008,
The Stranger, newspaper
article; acrylic and collage

→→ *Loves Me Not*, 2008,
personal work; acrylic
and collage

*"As far back as I can remember it's been faces for me. Every illustrator has that
thing they always doodled obsessively as a kid and for me it was faces. And clearly
it's still faces. Rendering faces just puts me in the zone where I can lose myself
and look at the clock three hours later and wonder how that happened."*

*„Solange ich mich erinnern kann, haben mich Gesichter beschäftigt. Jeder Illustrator hat doch als Kind
obsessiv irgendwas gekritzelt, und bei mir waren das eben Gesichter. Und das sind sie immer noch.
Wenn ich Gesichter darstelle, kann ich mich selbst verlieren. Nach drei Stunden schaue ich
auf die Uhr und wundere mich, wie das geschehen konnte."*

*« Aussi loin que je me souvienne, j'ai toujours été attirée par les visages. Chaque illustrateur était
obsédé par un certain thème étant enfant, et pour moi c'était les visages. À l'évidence, c'est toujours
d'actualité. Dessiner des visages me met dans un état où je peux me perdre, et regarder l'horloge
trois heures plus tard et me demander comment le temps a pu passer aussi vite. »*

↑ Portraits of contributors:
Cruger, Tricia, and Liebrock, 2007,
HOW, magazine article;
acrylic and collage

→ Jean-Paul Gaultier, 2007,
OUT, magazine article;
acrylic and collage

←← *Gibson Girl*, portrait of
unknown, 2009, Ringling
College of Art & Design;
acrylic and collage

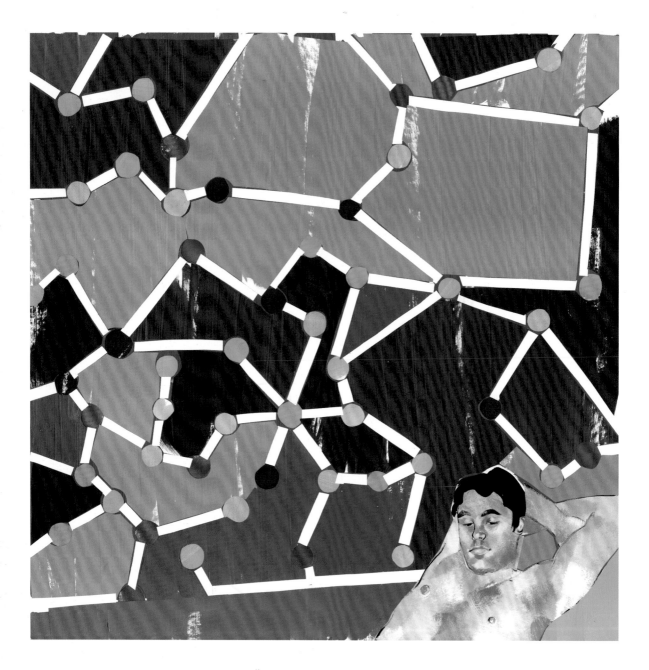

↑ *Lee Can't Sleep*, portrait of Lee Kohn, 2008,
personal work; acrylic and collage

→→ *Ohio Quotes*, portrait of Toni Morrison, Gloria
Steinem, Neil Armstrong, and the Wright Bros.,
2008, *Ohio* magazine; acrylic and collage

Anita Kunz

lives and works in Toronto (ON), Canada
www.anitakunz.com

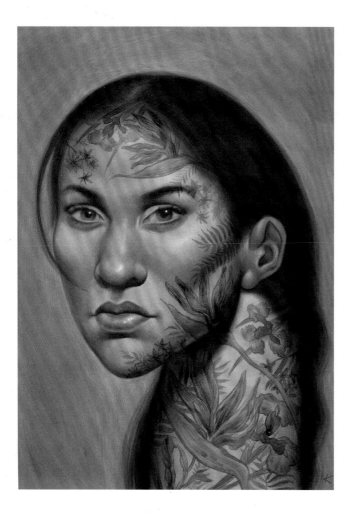

"It's always challenging capturing the person's likeness, mannerisms and characteristics but so much fun to create!"

„Es ist immer eine Herausforderung, die Ähnlichkeit einer Person einzufangen, ihre Eigenarten und Merkmale, und es macht unglaublich viel Freude, so etwas schöpferisch zu vollbringen!"

« C'est toujours difficile de rendre l'apparence, les traits et les caractéristiques du sujet, mais c'est tellement intéressant à créer ! »

↑   *J-Lo*, portrait of Jennifer Lopez, 2000, *Rolling Stone* magazine, magazine article; watercolour and gouache

→   *Madame Bovary redux*, portrait of Leonardo DiCaprio and Jennifer Love Hewitt, 1997, *Entertainment Weekly*, magazine article; watercolour and gouache

→→ Charles Darwin, 2009, The Illustration Academy, video instruction and demonstration; watercolour and gouache

↑   Elton John, 1998, *The New Yorker*,
magazine article; watercolour and gouache

→   Madonna, 1999, *Los Angeles* magazine,
article; mixed media

←← Cher, 1991, *Entertainment Weekly*,
magazine article; mixed media,
watercolour and collage

→→ Justin Bieber, 2010, *Rolling Stone* magazine,
article; watercolour and gouache

←   Stephen Hawking, 1999, *The LA Times*,
magazine article; watercolour and gouache

↓   *The year in movies*, portrait of Quentin Tarantino
and Tom Hanks, 2000, *Rolling Stone* magazine,
magazine article; watercolour and gouache

Rory Kurtz

lives and works in West Bend (WI), USA
www.rorykurtzillustration.com

AGENT
Levy Creative Management
www.levycreative.com

*"Portraits are for me an impression
of the individual, sometimes putting
them in the right environment,
a specific narrative, or focusing
on certain expressions."*

„Porträts sind für mich der Eindruck, den ein
Individuum macht. Manchmal wird es in die richtige
Umgebung gesetzt, in einen speziellen erzählerischen
Zusammenhang, oder man konzentriert sich auf
einen bestimmten Ausdruck."

« Pour moi, le portrait est une impression de l'individu,
qui se traduit en le situant dans l'environnement
ou l'histoire qui convient, ou en se concentrant
sur certaines expressions. »

↑   *Let the Right One In*, portrait of
Kare Hedebrant and Lina Leandersson,
2009, personal work; digital

→   Portrait of unknown, 2010, *Miami
New Times*, cover art/editorial; digital

→→ *Electra*, portrait of Vanessa Eggers,
2009, personal work, Creative Quarterly
Gold Medal; digital

↑   *Ironman Mark III*, portrait of Robert Downey Jr.,
2009, personal work; digital

←← *Waking With Wolves*, portrait of Melissa Lawent,
2009, personal work; digital

↑ *Bonne*, portrait of
unknown, 2009, personal
work; digital

←← Brad Bansemer, 2009,
personal work; digital

Lapin

lives and works in Barcelona, Spain
www.lesillustrationsdelapin.com

AGENT
VO Valérie Oualid
France
www.valerieoualid.com

*"Catching the intensity and
the emotions of friends' glances
has become a habit. I like
the intimacy of these moments
shared with the model."*

*„Es wurde mir zur Gewohnheit, die Intensität
und Emotionen der Blicke meiner Freunde
einzufangen. Mir gefällt die Intimität dieser
Momente, die ich mit dem Modell teile."*

*« Saisir l'intensité et les émotions des regards d'un
ami est devenu une habitude. J'aime l'intimité
de ces moments partagés avec le modèle. »*

↑   *I left my head in tokyo*, Lapin,
self-portrait, 2010, personal work;
hand drawing, watercolour, ink, pen

→   *Bipolar disorder*, 2009, Sadag, Grey
South Africa, advertising; hand drawing,
Adobe Photoshop

→→ Mélanie Pain, 2008, album cover;
hand drawing, watercolour, ink, pen,
Adobe Photoshop

↑ *Enchanté*, portrait of Julia, 2010,
personal work; hand drawing, watercolour,
ink, pen, Adobe Photoshop

← *Beijinhos*, portrait of Monica, 2010,
personal work; hand drawing, watercolour,
ink, pen, Adobe Photoshop

↓ *Wunderbar!!!*, portrait of Tine, 2010,
personal work; hand drawing, watercolour,
ink, pen, Adobe Photoshop

↑   *Cosplays*, portrait of Moka, 2010,
personal work, book; hand drawing,
watercolour, ink, pen

Daniel Lim

lives and works in Los Angeles (CA), USA
www.fawnfruits.com

"*I want to show beauty,
one fawn fruits at a time.*"

„*Ich will Schönheit zeigen, immer nur
ein schönes Gesicht zur selben Zeit.*"

«*Je veux montrer de la beauté,
fawn fruits après fawn fruits.* »

↑ *GladysEye*, portrait of Roxanne Kirigoe,
2007, series 1000 fawnfruits portraits;
colour pencil and acrylic on paper

→ *Misty Misia*, portrait of Misia, 2007,
series 1000 fawnfruits portraits; colour
pencil and acrylic on paper

→→ *So very Special*, portrait of someone very
special, 2007, series 1000 fawnfruits portraits;
acrylic and colour pencil on paper

↑ *27th of May*, portrait of Mitsuka
in Harajuku, 2009, Sweet Streets;
acrylic and colour pencil on canvas

→ *29th of August*, portrait of Lynn in
Harajuku, 2009, Mondo Bizzarro Gallery,
Rome; acrylic and colour pencil on canvas

←← *Butterflies for Annie*, 2007,
series 1000 fawnfruits portraits;
colour pencil and acrylic on paper

↑   *Waiting Winona*, 2008, personal work;
acrylic and colour pencil on wood

←← *Eimi*, 2010, Sweet Streets, exhibition;
acrylic and colour pencil on canvas

Pablo Lobato

lives and works in Buenos Aires, Argentina
http://lobaton.wordpress.com

AGENT
Anna Goodson
Management
www.agoodson.com

"I use 70% of the time to get to know the person I am portraying. And just 30% to draw them."

„70 % der Zeit brauche ich, um die Person kennenzulernen, die ich porträtiere. Und nur 30 %, um sie zu zeichnen."

« J'utilise 70 % du temps à apprendre à connaître la personne dont je fais le portrait. Et les 30 % restants à la dessiner. »

↑   Stevie Wonder, 2003, *Rolling Stone* magazine, magazine article; pencil, Adobe Illustrator, Adobe Photoshop

→   Rihanna, 2009, *Flare*, magazine article; pencil, Adobe Illustrator, Adobe Photoshop

→→ Julia Roberts, 2006, *Flare*, magazine article; pencil, Adobe Illustrator, Adobe Photoshop

↑ Bob Marley, 2009, AGM,
promotional coaster; pencil,
Adobe Illustrator, Adobe Photoshop

← Jimi Hendrix, 2007, *Rolling Stone*
magazine, article; pencil, Adobe
Illustrator, Adobe Photoshop

↑　Michael Jackson, 2004, *Essence*,
magazine article; pencil, Adobe Illustrator,
Adobe Photoshop

↖　James Brown, 2005, *Rolling Stone*
magazine, article; pencil, Adobe Illustrator,
Adobe Photoshop

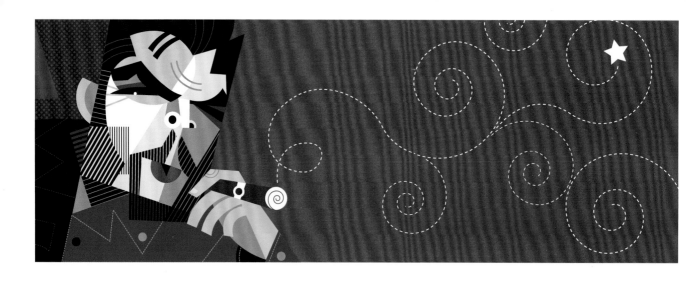

→ Karl Lagerfeld, 2007, *Flare*, magazine article; pencil, Adobe Illustrator, Adobe Photoshop

↓ Snoop Dogg, 2006, *Flare*, magazine article; pencil, Adobe Illustrator, Adobe Photoshop

←← *Che*, portrait of Ernesto "Che" Guevara, 2010, *Göoo Mag*, magazine article; pencil, Adobe Illustrator, Adobe Photoshop

→   Leonardo DiCaprio, 2007, *Flare*, magazine article; pencil, Adobe Illustrator, Adobe Photoshop

Liz Lomax

lives and works in Brooklyn (NY), USA
www.lizlomax.com

"I like to sculpt surreal portraits, distorting the subjects' features while still capturing their likeness, then photograph them for illustration."

„Ich forme gerne surreale Porträts: Dabei verzerre ich die Züge der Person, fange aber gleichzeitig auch ihre Gestalt ein. Dann fotografiere ich sie als Illustration."

« J'aime sculpter des portraits surréalistes, déformer les traits du sujet tout en conservant la ressemblance, puis les photographier pour en faire des illustrations. »

↑ Sweetie, the famous New York City drag queen, 2007,
Pure Content Pictures, movie poster; polymer clay,
oil paint, jewellery, glitter, digital photography

→ Kenny Chesney, 2007, *Nashville Scene*, magazine article;
polymer clay, oil paint, digital photography

→→ *The Perfect Storm*, portrait of Steve Jobs, 2008, University
of South Carolina, magazine article; polymer clay, oil paint,
insulation foam, digital photography

↑   50 Cent, 2004, *Rolling Stone* magazine, article; polymer clay,
oil paint, jewellery, fabric and fake fur, digital photography

→→ Mick Jagger, 2004, *Rolling Stone* magazine, article; polymer clay,
oil paint, jewellery, digital photography

↑   *Wardrobe Malfunction*, portrait of Janet
Jackson and Justin Timberlake, 2010,
Melcher Media, book; polymer clay,
oil paint, digital photography

←← Tiger Woods, 2006, *Golf Digest*,
magazine article; polymer clay, oil paint,
insulation foam, digital photography

Bob London

lives and works in London, UK
www.boblondon.co.uk

AGENT

VO Valérie Oualid
France
www.valerieoualid.com

2agenten
Berlin
www.2agenten.com

"Beautiful or grotesque, realistic or caricature, I am not limited by style or technique and treat each new face as a new adventure."

„Wunderschön oder grotesk, realistisch oder karikiert – ich bin auf keinen Stil und keine Technik festgelegt und behandele jedes neue Gesicht als neues Abenteuer."

« Beau ou grotesque, réaliste ou caricatural, je ne suis pas limité par le style ou la technique, et je traite chaque nouveau visage comme une nouvelle aventure. »

↑   Jim Newcombe, 2010, *Zine A*, book; hand drawing, Adobe Photoshop

→   *Marigold*, portrait of Daisy & Ginger, 2010, Graniph, T-shirt; hand drawing, Adobe Photoshop

→→ *Bob Rainbow*, Bob London, self-portrait, 2009, personal work; hand drawing, Adobe Photoshop

↑ *Mean Business*, portrait of George, Oscar, Nile & Terence,
2009, *Technology Review*, magazine editorial; hand drawing,
Adobe Photoshop

↑   Serge Gainsbourg, 2010, Portraits of Serge, website;
hand drawing, Adobe Photoshop

Nice Lopes

lives and works in Santos (SP), Brazil
www.nicelopes.blogspot.com

"Portraits have the power to uncover the soul like ghosts from the past that hypnotise anyone who dares to look at them."

„Porträts haben die Macht, die Seele aufzudecken – wie Geister aus der Vergangenheit, die jeden hypnotisieren, der es wagt, sie anzuschauen.“

« Les portraits ont le pouvoir de dévoiler l'âme, comme des fantômes du passé qui hypnotisent quiconque ose les regarder. »

↑   Amélie Poulain from the movie *The Fabulous Destiny of Amélie Poulain*, 2010, personal work, collective exhibition; CorelDraw, Adobe Photoshop, collage, hand drawing

→   Thom Yorke, 2010, personal work, collective exhibition; CorelDraw, Adobe Photoshop

→→ Chantal, 2008, personal work, calendar; CorelDraw, Adobe Photoshop, collage, hand drawing

Kristof Luyckx

lives and works in Ghent, Belgium
www.kristofluyckx.be

AGENT

VO Valérie Oualid
France
www.valerieoualid.com

Shop Around
The Netherlands
www.shop-around.nl

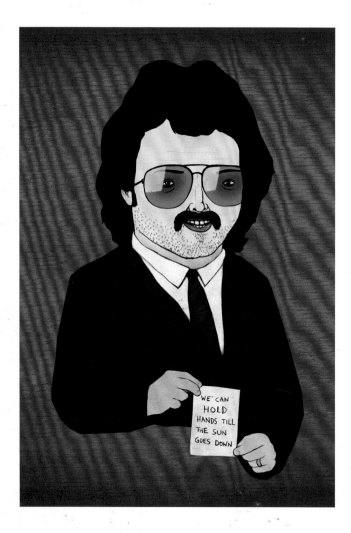

*"The portrayed character has
to reflect coolness or insecurity,
or foolishness."*

*„Der porträtierte Charakter muss Coolness,
Unsicherheit oder Dummheit widerspiegeln."*

*« Le personnage représenté doit dégager
de la désinvolture, un manque de confiance
en soi, ou de la sottise. »*

↑ Barry, 2007, personal work;
Adobe Photoshop

→ Wanda and Dirk, 2006,
personal work; Adobe Photoshop

→→ Herman Brusselmans, 2009,
Het Parool, newspaper article;
Adobe Photoshop

↑   *Soccers*, 2009, personal work,
exhibition; Adobe Photoshop

←← Eugene, 2009, *Vrij Nederland*,
magazine article; Adobe Photoshop

Francisco Martins

lives and works in Lisbon, Portugal
www.behance.net/francmartins

"Studying a face can be mesmerising for its expressions tell infinite stories. I try to go beyond physical likeness and aim to grasp people's essence."

„Das Studium eines Gesichts kann einen hypnotisieren, weil seine verschiedenen Ausdrücke unendlich viele Geschichten erzählen. Ich versuche, hinter die physische Ähnlichkeit zu kommen, und will die Essenz des Menschen erfassen."

« Étudier un visage peut être fascinant, car ses expressions racontent des histoires infinies. J'essaie d'aller au-delà de la ressemblance physique et de saisir l'essence des gens. »

↑   Francisco Martins, self-portrait, 2010, *DIF*, magazine article; Adobe Photoshop

→   Paul Bowles, 2010, *Umbigo*, magazine article; Adobe Photoshop

→→ Erykah Badu, 2010, personal work; Adobe Photoshop

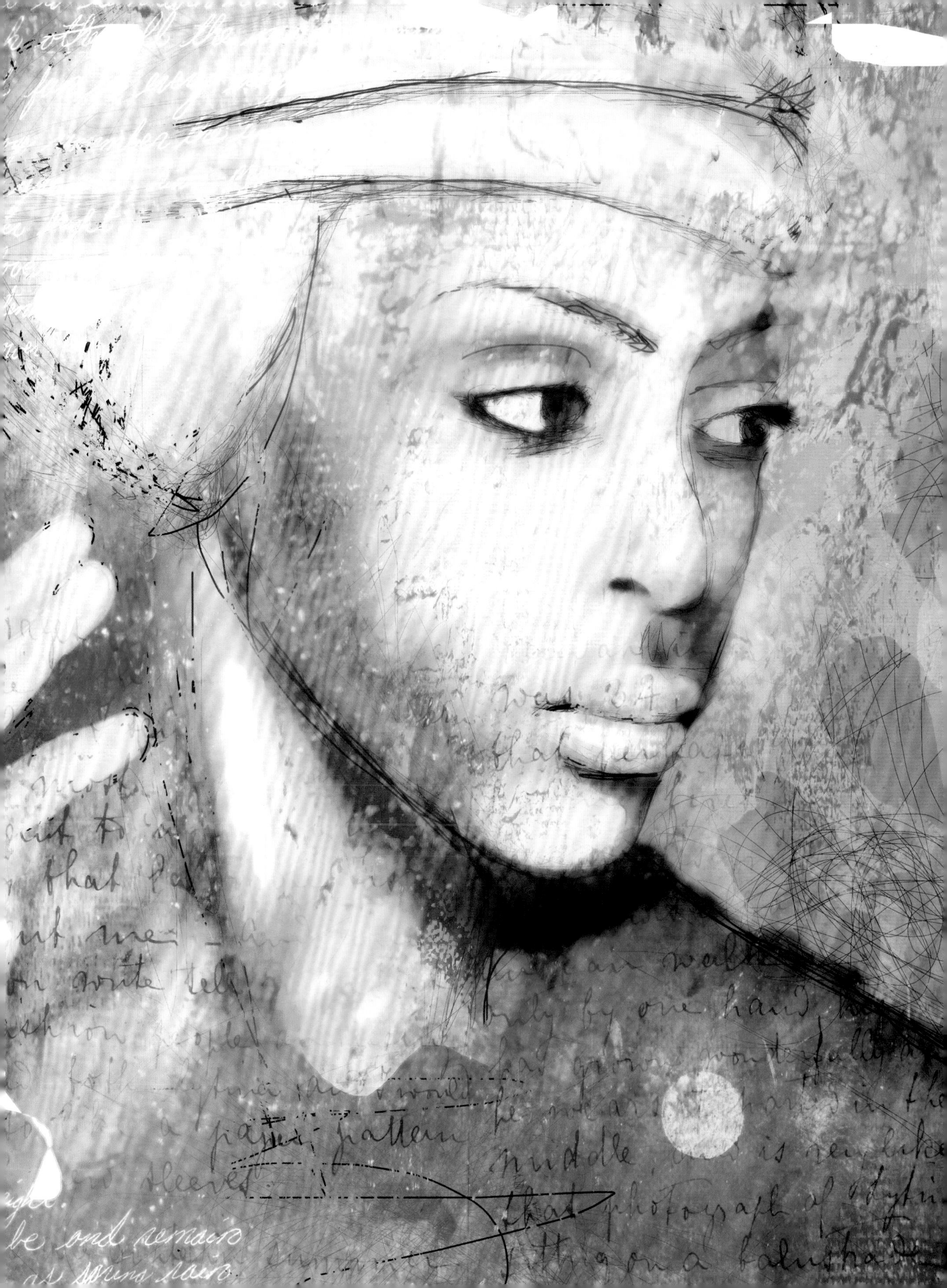
paper pattern
sleeves
be and remains

↑   Chico Buarque, 2010, personal work;
Adobe Photoshop

→   Tom Welling, 2010, personal work;
Adobe Photoshop

←← Gisele Bündchen, 2010, personal work;
Adobe Photoshop

Jorge Mascarenhas

lives and works in Alameda (CA), USA
www.jorgemstudio.com

AGENT
Levy Creative Management
www.levycreative.com

"As an illustrator, it is my job to give something that a photograph can't. One hopes that the result is a 'presence', as well as a likeness."

„Als Illustrator ist es mein Job, etwas zu geben, was ein Foto nicht vermitteln kann. Meine Hoffnung ist, dass das Ergebnis eine ‚Präsenz' ist und außerdem Ähnlichkeit aufweist."

« En tant qu'illustrateur, mon travail est de donner quelque chose qu'un photographe ne peut pas donner. J'espère que le résultat est un portrait fidèle auquel s'ajoute une ‹ présence ›. »

↑   *My friend Susana*, 2010, personal work; exhibition; oil and ink on board

→   *My friend Gabriela*, 2010, personal work; oil and ink on board

→→ Emma Watson as Hermione Granger, 2010, personal work; oil and ink on board

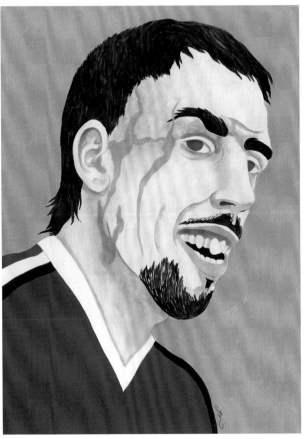

↑   Natalie Portman as Anne Boleyn
in the movie *The Other Boleyn Girl*, 2010,
personal work; oil and ink on board

←← *World Cup Hunks*, portraits of Carlos
Tevez, Wayne Rooney, Carles Puyol and
Franck Ribéry, 2010, personal work;
oil and ink on board

Mone Maurer

lives and works in Wallhausen, Germany
www.monemaurer.com

"I love this quote: 'so much is cheesy and that's for sheezy but with melodies like these I'll make it easy peasy.' "

„Ich liebe diese Liedzeile: ‚So much is cheesy and that's for sheezy but with melodies like these I'll make it easy peasy.'"

«J'adore cette citation : ‹ So much is cheesy and that's for sheezy but with melodies like these I'll make it easy peasy. ›»

— Chilly Gonzales

↑   *Recover Beauty*, portrait of Claudia Schiffer, 2007, *Vorn* magazine #4, editorial; mixed media

→   *This is Michael*, portrait of Michael Jackson, 2009, *+rosebud* magazine #07, magazine editorial; mixed media

→→ *Dead Rockers*, portrait of Jim Morrison, 2008, *Indie* magazine #21, magazine editorial; mixed media

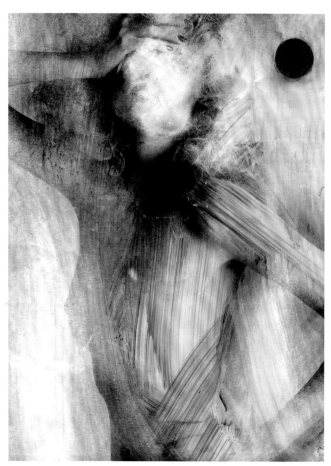

↑ *Recover Privacy #1* and *Recover Privacy #2*, 2008, *Rojo* magazine, issue *Egal*, magazine editorial; mixed media

→→ Moses Pelham, rapper and label owner, 2010, *Aortica* magazine, editorial; mixed media

Jason Mecier

lives and works in San Francisco (CA), USA
www.jasonmecier.com

AGENT
Munro Campagna
www.munrocampagna.com

"I love to create amazing 3-D mosaic portraits of pop culture icons from objects such as make-up, candy, pills, food, and celebrities' actual junk!"

„Ich schaffe gerne verblüffende Mosaikporträts in 3-D von Ikonen der Popkultur aus solchen Objekten wie Make-up, Süßigkeiten, Pillen, Speisen oder auch Abfall dieser Prominenten!"

« J'adore créer des portraits étonnants d'icônes de la culture pop en fabriquant des mosaïques en 3D à partir d'objets tels que du maquillage, des bonbons, des pilules, de la nourriture, et les ordures des peoples ! »

↑ Mary-Louise Parker, 2010, personal work; mixed media on panel; this piece includes some of Mary-Louise Parker's personal items

→ Stevie Nicks, 2009, personal work; mixed media on panel

→→ Nicolas Cage, 2010, personal work; mixed media on panel

↑ *Ripley's Believe it or Not!*, Taylor Swift, 2010; 1000 Good & Plenty candies glued on board

→ Courtney Love, 2010, *Glamour* UK, magazine article; pills glued on board

→→ Heath Ledger, 2010, *Glamour* UK, magazine article; pills glued on board

↑ *RuPaul's Drag Race*, RuPaul, 2009,
Bizarre, magazine article; mixed media on
panel; this piece includes some of RuPaul's
personal items

←← *Chelsea Handler*, 2010, Live Nation,
poster for Chelsea's *2010 Chelsea Chelsea
Bang Bang Tour*; mixed media on panel

Gildo Medina

lives and works in Paris, France
www.gildomedina.com

AGENT

Galerie 13 Jeannette
Mariani, Paris
www.galerie13jm.com

Serlin Associates
London
www.serlinassociates.com

Art Department
New York
www.art-dept.com

"To make portraits involves a seductive relationship between the selfish point of view of the model, and my own selfish view of beauty, then the game begins."

„Zur Porträtmalerei gehört eine verführerische Beziehung zwischen dem selbstbezogenen Standpunkt des Modells und meiner eigenen selbstsüchtigen Betrachtungsweise von Schönheit. Damit beginnt das Spiel."

« Le portrait implique une relation de séduction entre le point de vue égoïste du modèle, et ma propre vision égoïste de la beauté. C'est là que le jeu commence. »

↑ *Fashion Victim*, portrait of Alexander McQueen, 2010, *Next Libération*, Paris, magazine article; pencil drawing, watercolour on paper

→ *Fashion Victim*, portrait of Daul Kim, 2010, *Next Libération*, Paris, magazine article; pencil drawing, watercolour on paper

→→ *Fashion Victim*, portrait of Isabella Blow, 2010, *Next Libération*, Paris, magazine article; pencil drawing, watercolour on paper

↑   German DJs, 2006, *Hekmag*,
magazine article; pencil drawing,
watercolour and marker on paper

←← Le Mat, 2010, Galerie 13 Jeannette
Mariani, Paris; pencil drawing,
watercolour and ink on paper

KIM JONG-IL

→→ *Madrid, el secreto encanto*, portrait of Ana Amaya, 2009, *El Palacio de Hierro*, magazine cover; pencil drawing, watercolour and pen on paper

← *Le mur du pouvoir*, portrait of Kim Jong-il, 2006, *Which*, magazine article; pencil drawing, watercolour and pen on paper

↓ *The Trinity. Sad, Empty, Poor*, 2010, Manuel Landa; pencil drawing, watercolour and pen on paper

Mari Mitsumi

lives and works in Yokohama (Kanagawa), Japan
http://home.att.ne.jp/green/mari-m

"I always try to seek and depict something between individuality and universality through the eyes of my models which reflect the light and shade in their spirit."

„Ich bin stets auf der Suche danach, etwas zwischen Individualität und Universalität durch die Augen meiner Modelle darzustellen, die das Licht und den Schatten ihrer Seele reflektieren."

« J'essaie toujours de chercher et de représenter quelque chose entre l'individualité et l'universalité à travers les yeux de mes modèles, qui reflètent la lumière et l'ombre de leur esprit. »

↑   *Penumbra variation*, 2010, personal work, gallery show; acrylic paint on canvas, Adobe Photoshop

→   *Next to silence*, 2008, personal work, gallery show; acrylic paint on canvas, Adobe Photoshop

→→ *Anemones*, 2008, personal work, gallery show; acrylic paint on canvas

↑　*April/March*, 2008, personal work,
gallery show; acrylic paint on canvas

→　*Twinkle*, 2008, personal work,
gallery show; acrylic paint on canvas

→→ *It's all in your mind*, 2008, personal
work, gallery show; acrylic paint on canvas

↑   *The Little Prince and His Rose*,
2009, personal work, gallery show;
acrylic paint on canvas

→→ *100 days off*, 2008, personal work,
gallery show; acrylic paint on canvas

Joe Morse

lives and works in Toronto (ON), Canada
www.joemorse.com

AGENT

Heflinreps
New York
www.heflinreps.com

Killington Arts
UK
www.killingtonarts.com

"I work with the public face of celebrities, so my aim in every portrait is to reveal the person hiding behind the curtain."

„Ich arbeite mit dem öffentlichen Gesicht der Prominenten. Also ziele ich in jedem Porträt darauf ab, die Person zu enthüllen, die sich hinter dem Vorhang versteckt."

« Je travaille avec les visages publics des célébrités, donc, dans chaque portrait, mon objectif est de révéler la personne qui se cache derrière le rideau. »

↑   *A Star is Born*, portrait of Vladimir Putin, 2006, *The New Republic*, magazine cover; oil and acrylic on paper

→   Lance Armstrong, 2004, *ESPN*, magazine article; oil and acrylic on paper

→→ Hilary Swank, 2006, *Premiere*, magazine article; oil and acrylic on paper

↑   *Ego Trippin*, portrait of Snoop Dogg, 2008,
Rolling Stone magazine, album review; oil and
acrylic on paper

←← *Malcolm X*, portrait of Denzel Washington, 2007,
Premiere, magazine article; oil and acrylic on paper

→→ *Working Class Boy to Man U*, portrait of David Beckham, 2007, *Los Angeles Times*, newspaper article; oil and acrylic on paper

↓ *Sopranos*, portrait of James Gandolfini, 2007, *San Francisco Chronicle*, newspaper article; oil and acrylic on paper

↑ *Soul*, portrait of Isaac Hayes, 2010, personal work; oil and acrylic on paper

↓ Pearl Jam, 2006, *Rolling Stone* magazine, magazine article; oil and acrylic on paper

Fumi Nakamura

lives and works in Brooklyn (NY), USA
www.miniminiaturemouse.com

"It is not only about illustrating the characteristics of faces, but also capturing the moments, emotions, and story about that person."

„Es geht nicht nur um die Abbildung der Eigenarten von Gesichtern, sondern auch darum, Augenblicke, Gefühle und Geschichten über diese Person einzufangen."

« Il ne s'agit pas seulement d'illustrer les caractéristiques des visages, mais aussi de saisir les moments, les émotions et l'histoire de cette personne. »

↑ *Hidden Place*, portrait of Björk, 2008, personal work; hand drawing, colour pencil, graphite

→→ *This Will Destroy You!*, portrait of Christopher Royal King, 2010, personal work; hand drawing, colour pencil, graphite

↑ Blue Rose, 2009, *Nylon*, magazine article;
hand drawing, colour pencil, graphite

→ Jay Jay Pistolet, 2009, *Nylon*, magazine article;
hand drawing, colour pencil, graphite

↑   Mumford & Sons, 2009, *Nylon*, magazine article;
hand drawing, colour pencil, graphite

Patricio Oliver

lives and works in Buenos Aires, Argentina
www.patriciooliver.com.ar

*"A portrait is a reflection of
the portrayed character's
most distinctive traits
tinged with some aspects
of my personality."*

*„Ein Porträt ist die Reflexion der
hervorstechendsten Eigenschaften
der porträtierten Person, gefärbt
von einigen Aspekten meiner
eigenen Persönlichkeit."*

*« Un portrait est un reflet des traits
les plus caractéristiques du sujet,
teintés par certains aspects
de ma personnalité. »*

← *Thom in Rain BOWS*, portrait of Thom Yorke,
2007, *Rolling Stone* magazine, Argentina, article;
Illustrator Wacom Tablet, Adobe Photoshop

→→ Mujercitas Terror, 2010, Mujercitas Terror band,
e-flyer; Illustrator Wacom Tablet, Adobe Photoshop

→→ *Forever Together*, portrait of Fidel Nadal,
2010, *Rolling Stone* magazine, Argentina, article;
Illustrator Wacom Tablet, Adobe Photoshop

← *Occa Facone*, 2009, personal work;
Illustrator Wacom Tablet, Adobe Photoshop

↓ *Mediumship*, 2009, Centro Cultural
de España Santiago Chile, exhibition;
Illustrator Wacom Tablet, Adobe Photoshop

Roberto Parada

lives and works in Annapolis (MD), USA
www.robertoparada.com

*"I bring a painterly
approach to my portraits
and I'm always seeking
to capture the essence of
the subject in their likeness."*

*„Ich gehe meine Porträts auf
malerische Weise an und versuche
stets, das Wesen des Subjekts in
seiner Gestalt abzubilden."*

*« J'approche mes portraits comme
un peintre, et je cherche toujours
à saisir l'essence du sujet dans
sa représentation physique. »*

↑   Elvis Costello, 2005, *Rolling Stone*
magazine, article; oil on linen

→   Cate Blanchett as Bob Dylan in the
movie *I'm Not There*, 2007, *Entertainment
Weekly*, magazine article; oil on linen

→→ *A Remembrance*, portrait of Ahmet
Ertegun, founder of Atlantic Records,
2008, *Billboard*, magazine article;
oil on linen

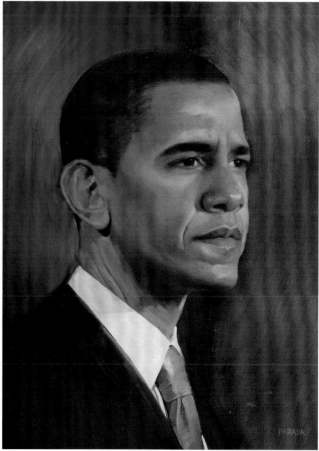

↑   George W. Bush, 2008, *Newsweek*,
magazine article; oil on linen

→   *President Elect*, portrait of Barack
Obama, 2008, *Newsweek*, magazine article;
oil on linen

←←   *Tony Soprano*, portrait of James
Gandolfini, 2007, *New York* magazine,
article; oil on linen

↑   *Time's 100 Most Influential People*
2005, portrait of Jon Stewart, 2005,
Time magazine, article; oil on linen

→ *Time's 100 Most Influential People 2005*, portrait of Clint Eastwood, 2005, *Time* magazine, article; oil on linen

↘ Timothy Geithner, U.S. Secretary of the Treasury, 2009, *Business Week*, magazine article; oil on linen

↓ Gore Vidal, 2007, *The LA Times*, magazine article; oil on linen

Susanne Paschke

lives and works in Berlin, Germany
www.susannepaschke.de

"I try to invite the viewer to see beyond the subject matter of my work, into a world of super brilliant colours, tones, and patterns."

„Ich will den Betrachter einladen, über das Greifbare meiner Arbeit hinaus zu schauen in eine Welt der überirdisch brillanten Farben, Schattierungen und Muster."

« J'essaie d'inviter le spectateur à voir au-delà du sujet de mon œuvre, dans un monde de couleurs, tons et motifs extrêmement vifs. »

↑   Eva Longoria, 2010, personal work, poster; Adobe Illustrator

→   Beyoncé, 2006, personal work, poster; Adobe Illustrator

→→ Illa J., 2009, personal work; Adobe Illustrator

Stina Persson

lives and works in Stockholm, Sweden
www.stinapersson.com

AGENT

CWC International
New York
www.cwc-i.com

CWC Tokyo
Japan
www.cwctokyo.com

Agent Bauer
Stockholm
www.agentbauer.com

*"It is all about the eyes. And as little
as possible about smiles and teeth.
Sometimes it becomes more a portrait
of a hairdo or a sweater. And that's ok."*

„Es geht vor allem um die Augen. Und nur so wenig wie
möglich um das Lächeln und die Zähne. Manchmal
wird es mehr zu einem Porträt der Frisur oder
des Pullovers. Und das ist okay.“

« Pour moi, tout se passe dans les yeux. Et aussi peu
que possible dans les sourires et les dents. Parfois,
cela devient le portrait d›une coiffure ou d'un vêtement.
C'est très bien comme ça. »

↑   Modern Tippi Hedren, 2010, Gallery Hanahou,
New York, show "Perfectly Flawed"; watercolour, cut paper

→   *Who Doesn't Love a Girl who Smells Like Tangerine?*,
portrait of Johanna S., 2010, Gallery Hanahou, New York,
show "Perfectly Flawed"; watercolour, cut paper

→→ Tina, 2010, Gallery Hanahou, New York, show
"Perfectly Flawed"; watercolour, cut plastic bag, India ink

←← Penélope Cruz, 2010, *Latina* magazine,
editorial; watercolour, Adobe Photoshop

→ *Loretta*, 2010, Gallery Hanahou, New York,
show "Perfectly Flawed"; watercolour, plastic film

↓ *String of Pearls*, portrait of Magda,
2010, Gallery Hanahou, New York, show
"Perfectly Flawed"; watercolour and frisket

Dominic Philibert

lives and works in Montreal (Québec), Canada
http://dominicphilibert.blogspot.com

"When I'm drawing or painting a portrait, I try to capture the essence of the subject by emphasising the authenticity of their own unique personality."

„Wenn ich ein Porträt zeichne oder male, versuche ich, das Innerste des Subjekts im Bild zu erfassen, indem ich die Authentizität seiner eigenen einzigartigen Persönlichkeit betone."

« Lorsque je dessine ou peins un portrait, j'essaie de saisir l'essence du sujet en soulignant l'authenticité de sa personnalité propre. »

↑   Lady Gaga, 2010, *Le Samedi*, magazine article; digital

→   Susan Boyle, 2010, *Le Samedi*, magazine article; digital

→→ Bob Dylan, 2008, personal work; digital

↑   Woody Allen, 2009, personal work; digital

←← Brad Pitt, 2010, *Le Samedi*, magazine article; digital

→ → Donald Trump, 2010, CLARKtoys,
online video game trailer; digital

← *The Mad'Onna Hatter*, portrait of Madonna,
2009, *XFuns*, magazine cover; digital

↙ Ozzy Osbourne, 2008, personal work; digital

↓ Benicio Del Toro, 2009, personal work; digital

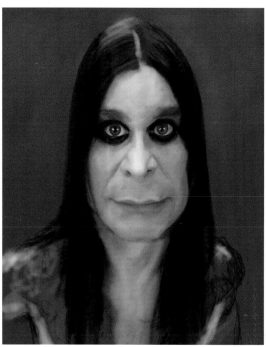

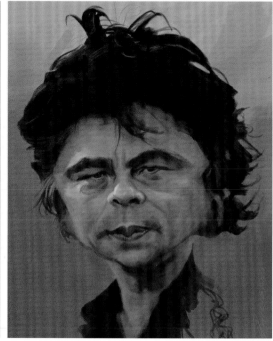

Hanoch Piven

lives and works in Barcelona, Spain and Tel Aviv, Israel
www.pivenworld.com

AGENT
Heflinreps
www.heflinreps.com

*"Making a portrait with objects
is for me a process which involves
looking, drawing, painting,
trial and error, serendipity,
and above all playing!"*

„Wenn ich aus Objekten ein Porträt erstelle,
ist das für mich ein Prozess, zu dem Beobachten,
Zeichnen, Malen, Versuch und Irrtum, glückliche
Zufälle und vor allem Spielen gehören!"

« Faire un portrait avec des objets est pour
moi un processus qui implique le regard,
le dessin, la peinture, l'essai et l'erreur,
le hasard, et surtout le jeu ! »

↑   Stephen Hawking, 2006,
Die Weltwoche, magazine article; collage

→   Keith Richards, 2008, *Spin*,
magazine article; collage

→→ Sacha Baron Cohen as Borat, 2007,
The Village Voice, newspaper article; collage

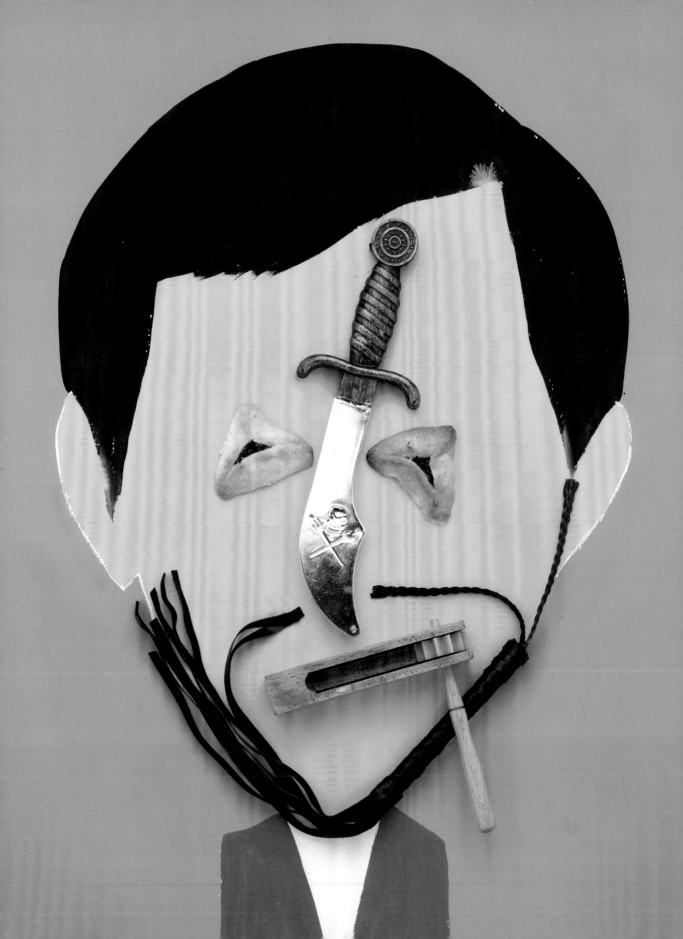

←← Mahmoud Ahmadinejad, 2008, *Maariv*, newspaper article; collage

→ Kim Jong-il, 2006, *Time* magazine, article; collage

↘ Fidel Castro, 1996, *Haaretz*, newspaper article; collage

↓ Barack Obama, 2009, *Esquire*, magazine article; collage

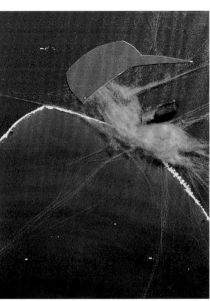

↑   Karl Marx, 2009, *Foreign Report*,
magazine article; collage

→   Sigmund Freud, 2002, *Haaretz*,
newspaper article; collage

→→ Charles Darwin, 2010, *Foreign
Report*, magazine article; collage

Wendy Plovmand

lives and works in London, UK, and Copenhagen, Denmark
www.wendyplovmand.com

AGENT
Central Illustration Agency   Traffic
London   New York
www.centralillustration.com   www.trafficnyc.com

"*My work is playful and fashionable in a pop-expressionistic way. I'm interested in mirroring both the beauty and the compelling otherness in human nature!*"

„*Meine Arbeiten sind verspielt und elegant auf eine pop-expressionistische Weise. Mich interessiert es, sowohl die Schönheit als auch die unwiderstehliche Andersartigkeit der menschlichen Natur zu spiegeln!*"

« *Mon travail est ludique et branché, sur un mode pop-expressionniste. Ce qui m'intéresse, c'est de refléter la beauté et la fascinante altérité de la nature humaine!* »

↑   Alexander McQueen, 2010, personal work; pencil, watercolour, Adobe Photoshop

→→ *Shopping crisis*, 2008, *Eurowoman* magazine; pencil, pen, watercolour, Adobe Photoshop

Edel Rodriguez

lives and works in Mount Tabor (NJ), USA
www.edelrodriguez.com

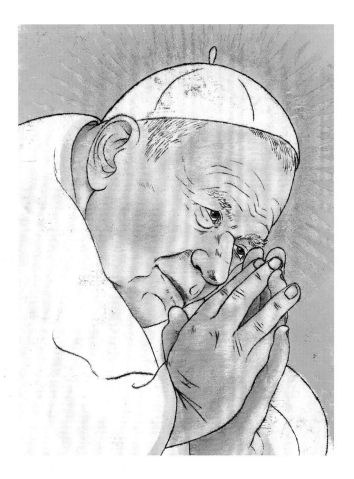

"I try to get at the essence of the subject in a clear and concise manner and often include biographical details that help inform the viewer."

„Ich versuche, auf klare und prägnante Weise zum Wesen des Subjekts vorzudringen, und nehme oft biografische Details mit auf, die dem Betrachter mehr verraten."

« J'essaie de saisir l'essence du sujet avec clarté et concision, et j'inclus souvent des détails biographiques qui informent le spectateur. »

↑   Pope John Paul II, 2004, *Time* magazine, article; pastel and ink on paper

→   Arthur Russell, 2005, *Time* magazine, article; mixed media

→→ Melvin Van Peebles, 2006, *The New Yorker*, magazine article; mixed media

↑ Raul Castro, 2006, *Time* magazine,
article; monoprints, digital

→ Osama Bin Laden, 2006, *Time* magazine, article; pastel on papyrus

↘ *Nixon in China*, portrait of Richard Nixon and Mao Tse-Tung, 2009, Vancouver Opera, poster; acrylic on paper

↓ Joseph Stalin, 2007, *Time* magazine, article; pastel on paper

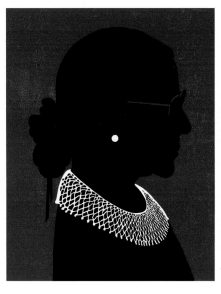

← Al Sharpton, 2007, *The New Republic*, magazine cover; mixed media

→→ Ray Barretto, 2008, *The New Yorker*, magazine article; acrylic on paper

↑ Judge Ruth Bader Ginsburg, 2009, *The New York Times*, magazine article; mixed media

↘ James Gandolfini as Tony Soprano, 2007, *The LA Times*, newspaper article; acrylic on paper

Paula Sanz Caballero

lives and works in Valencia, Spain
www.paulasanzcaballero.com

"I am always true to my figurative, detail-oriented style, of high-society figures in elegant, sophisticated surroundings, loaded with irony, dark humour and unsettling details that hint at deeper meanings below the polished surface."

„Ich bleibe meinem figürlichen, detailorientierten Stil immer treu, mit seinen Figuren der High Society, die sich in einer eleganten, kultivierten Umgebung befinden – alles ist voller Ironie, schwarzem Humor und beunruhigenden Details, die tiefere Bedeutungsebenen hinter der polierten Oberfläche andeuten."

« Je suis toujours fidèle à mon style figuratif et très détaillé, avec des personnages de la haute société dans des décors élégants et sophistiqués, chargés d'ironie, d'humour noir et de détails troublants qui révèlent des interprétations plus profondes sous la surface lisse. »

↑　*Barcelona*, 2010, Inditex, Spain, book; hand-stitched illustration

→→　*Catwalk*, 2008, Neiman Marcus, USA, book cover; hand-stitched illustration

↑   Portrait of unknown, 2004, Flowers Central
art gallery, London; hand-stitched illustration

←← *Corset*, 2006, Fashion DNA, Rijksmuseum,
Amsterdam, magazine article; hand-stitched illustration

Henriette Sauvant

lives and works in Hamburg, Germany
www.henriettesauvant.de

> "*Doing a portrait is like
> creating a small world around
> an invented person. Later,
> it seems to be an old friend.*"

> „*Porträtieren ist wie das Schaffen einer
> kleinen Welt um eine erfundene Person herum.
> Später erscheint sie wie ein alter Freund.*"

> «*Faire un portrait, c'est comme créer un petit
> monde autour d'une personne inventée.
> Plus tard, il semble s›agir d'un vieil ami.*»

↑ *Der Ozean des Mondes*, portrait of Jamila
Gavin, 2005, Ravensburger Verlag, book cover;
acrylic and oil colour on paper

→ *Kimberley Heuston: Antonia, Dantes
Tochter*, 2006, S. Fischer Verlag, book cover;
acrylic and oil colour on paper

→→ *Mirjam Pressler: Wundertütentage*, 2005,
Verlag Beltz & Gelberg, book cover; digital

↑ *Donna Jo Napoli: Donata, Tochter Venedigs*,
2005, S. Fischer Verlag, book cover; acrylic
and oil colour on paper

→ *Elizabeth E. Wein: Der Winterprinz*, 1998,
Deutscher Taschenbuch Verlag, dtv junior,
book cover; acrylic and oil colour on paper

→→ *Mirjam Pressler: Wenn das Glück kommt...*,
2004, Verlag Beltz & Gelberg, book cover;
acrylic and oil colour on paper

Helen Schiffer

lives and works in Frankfurt, Germany
www.helenschiffer.de

"In illustrations, I'm inspired by the elusive, unreasonable, unexpected – and by paradoxical comparisons."

„In der Illustration begeistert mich das Flüchtige, Unvernünftige, Unerwartete – und die paradoxen Gegenüberstellungen."

« Dans les illustrations, je suis inspiré par ce qui est élusif, déraisonnable, inattendu – et par les comparaisons paradoxales. »

↑   Jens Lehmann, 2010, personal work;
hand drawing, ink on paper

→   Patrick Owomoyela, 2010, personal
work; hand drawing, ink on paper

→→ Michael Ballack, 2010, personal work;
hand drawing, ink on paper

Rinat Shingareev

lives and works in Brescia, Italy
www.facebook.com/thebestartistalive

"I'm an observer who comments on everything that surrounds him, turning this mix of saturated colours and familiar personalities into pop art iconography."

„*Ich bin ein Beobachter, der alles in seiner Umgebung kommentiert und diese Mischung satter Farben und vertrauter Personen in eine Pop-Art-Ikonografie verwandelt.*"

« *Je suis un observateur qui commente tout ce qui l'entoure, et transforme ce mélange de couleurs saturées et de personnalités familières en iconographie pop art.* »

↑   Prince William, 2010,
personal work; oil on canvas

→   Lapo Elkann, 2008,
personal work; oil on canvas

→→ Michelle Hunziker, 2008,
personal work; oil on canvas

↑ *Cosmic Bush*, George W. Bush,
2010, personal work; oil on canvas

→→ Silvio Berlusconi, 2010,
personal work; oil on canvas

↑   Barack Obama, 2009,
personal work; oil on canvas

→   Nicolas Sarkozy, 2008,
personal work; oil on canvas

←← Roman Abramovich, 2008,
personal work; oil on canvas

Mariana Silva

lives and works in Mexico City, Mexico
www.marianasilva.com

"I like to take the person into an imaginary world, full of colours and lights. The more textures I use the closer I get to their state of mind."

„Ich nehme die Person gerne mit in eine imaginäre Welt voller Farben und Licht. Je mehr Texturen ich einsetze, desto näher komme ich ihrer seelischen Verfassung."

« J'aime emmener la personne dans un monde imaginaire, rempli de couleurs et de lumières. Plus j'utilise de textures, plus je m'approche de son état d'esprit. »

↑ *Mary*, 2010, personal work; Adobe Photoshop, Adobe Illustrator, watercolour

→ *Pop Girl*, 2010, personal work; Adobe Photoshop, Adobe Illustrator, watercolour

→→ *Ephemeral II*, 2008, *Pixel Society* magazine; Adobe Photoshop, Adobe Illustrator, watercolour

Cristiano Siqueira

lives and works in São Paulo, Brazil
www.crisvector.com

AGENT
Erika Groeschel
www.erikaillustrations.com

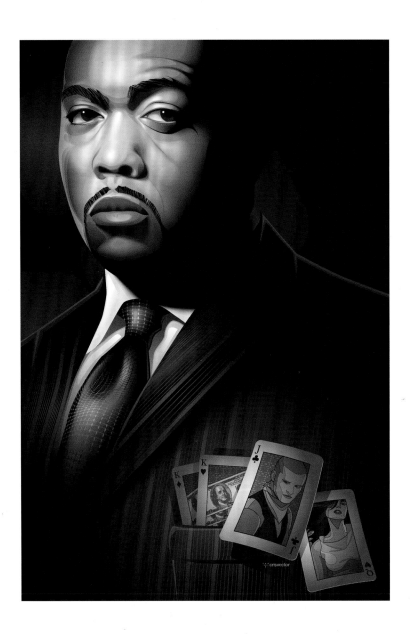

"My inspiration comes from traditional portraits but, in my works, I always try to give a modern touch and add more information about the person portrayed."

„Ich lasse mich von traditionellen Porträts inspirieren, doch in meinen Arbeiten versuche ich immer, sie moderner wirken zu lassen, und füge weitere Infos über die dargestellte Person hinzu."

« Mon inspiration vient des portraits traditionnels mais, dans mes œuvres, j'essaie toujours de donner une touche de modernité et d'ajouter des informations sur la personne représentée. »

← Timbaland, 2007, *Bizz* magazine, Editora Abril, article; Adobe Illustrator

→→ Leonard Mlodinow, physicist, 2009, *Galileu* magazine, Editora Globo, article; Adobe Illustrator

←← Lionel Messi, 2010, personal work; Adobe Illustrator

→ Lisa Shelley, 2008, personal work; Adobe Illustrator

↓ *Mrs. Morphine*, portrait of Miz, VirginPunk, 2007, personal work; Adobe Illustrator

Deanna Staffo

lives and works in Philadelphia (PA), USA
www.deannastaffo.com

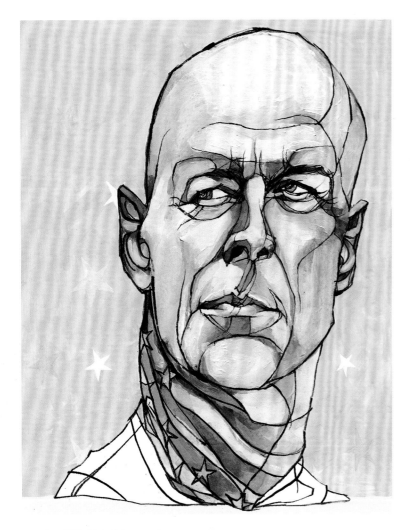

"Faces are endlessly inspiring to me because they come in so many different shapes and sizes and can change with the flick of a simple expression."

„Gesichter sind für mich endlos inspirierend, weil sie in Form und Größe so unterschiedlich sind und sich vom Ausdruck her innerhalb eines Augenblicks grundlegend verändern können."

« Les visages sont pour moi une source d'inspiration infinie parce qu'ils sont tous si différents, et une simple expression peut les transformer. »

↑ *Yippee Ki Yay Motherfucker*, portrait of Bruce Willis as John McClane from *Die Hard*, 2008, Slate.com, website; charcoal and acrylic

→ *Howl*, portrait of Allen Ginsberg, 2007, *The Baltimore City Paper*, newspaper article; charcoal

→→ Sofia Coppola, 2010, personal work; charcoal and acrylic

↑ Britt Daniel of the band Spoon,
2007, *The Baltimore City Paper*,
newspaper article; charcoal

→ Dusty Springfield, 2009,
The Baltimore City Paper,
newspaper article; charcoal

→→ *Harajuku Gwen*, portrait of
Gwen Stefani, 2006, personal work;
charcoal and acrylic

←← J.D. Salinger, 2010, personal work; charcoal and acrylic

↓ *Fast Times at Ridgemont High*, portrait of Brad Hamilton, 2006, personal work, trading card; charcoal and acrylic

↑ *Kanye vs. 50 Cent*, portrait of Kanye West and 50 Cent, 2007, *L.A. Weekly*, magazine article; charcoal and acrylic

↓ Data from the movie *The Goonies*, 2006, personal work, trading card; charcoal and acrylic

Fast Times at Ridgemont High   The Goonies

Dugald Stermer

lives and works in San Francisco (CA), USA
www.dugaldstermer.com

← John McPhee, 2006, *New York Times Book Review*, magazine article; pencil and watercolour on Arches watercolour paper

→→ Marianne Moore, 2005, *New York Times Book Review*, magazine article; coloured pencil on textured black paper

"I try and look for the characteristic most appealing to me. It doesn't have to be a physical one; it could be a matter of intellect, humor, or forcefulness. I don't know whether any of these factors come across in the final illustration, but that's where I start. When painting, I also usually start with the eyes, and work out from there."

„Ich mache mich auf die Suche nach den Merkmalen, die mich am meisten ansprechen. Das muss nicht unbedingt ein körperliches Merkmal sein, sondern kann auch zum Intellekt gehören oder etwas mit Humor oder Eindringlichkeit zu tun haben. Ob einige dieser Faktoren auch in der fertigen Illustration spürbar sind, weiß ich nicht, aber so fange ich jedenfalls an. Beim Malen beginne ich gewöhnlich mit den Augen und arbeite mich von dort weiter vor."

« J'essaie de chercher les caractéristiques qui me plaisent le plus. Ce n'est pas forcément physique, cela peut être une question d'intellect, d'humour ou de détermination. Je ne sais pas si ces facteurs transparaissent dans l'illustration finale, mais c'est sur eux que je me base. Lorsque je peins, en général que commence par les yeux. »

←← Brad Holland, 2005, *Graphis*,
magazine article; coloured pencil
on textured black paper

→ Herman Melville, Fyodor Dostoevsky,
Gustave Flaubert, 2002, *Los Angeles Times
Book Review*, magazine article; coloured
pencil on textured black paper

↘ Dante Alighieri, 2002, *New York Times
Book Review*, magazine article; coloured
pencil on textured black paper

↓ Meriwether Lewis and William Clark,
2004, *Time* magazine, article; coloured
pencil on textured black paper

↑ Rupert Sheldrake, 2000, *Utne Reader*, magazine article; pencil and watercolour on Arches watercolour paper

↗ *2020*, Dugald Stermer, self-portrait, 1999, *Mother Jones*, magazine article; pencil and watercolour on Arches watercolour paper

→ Sarah Turnbull, 2003, *Issue*, magazine article; pencil and watercolour on Arches watercolour paper

→→ Joe Louis, 1985, *Chicago* magazine, article; pencil and watercolour on Arches watercolour paper

JOE LOUIS

Ella Tjader

lives and works in Zurich, Switzerland
www.artlaundry.com

AGENT
Illustration Ltd
www.illustrationweb.com

"I like drawing pretty, gorgeous, and beautiful people. Mainly girls, because I can go a bit wilder with colours, shapes, and forms."

„Ich zeichne gerne hübsche, hinreißende und schöne Menschen. Vor allem Mädchen, weil ich da mit Farben, Formen und Gestalten etwas wilder sein kann."

« J'aime dessiner de beaux physiques. Surtout des filles, parce que les formes et les couleurs peuvent être plus extravagantes. »

↑   *Vera*, 2006, editorial and T-shirts design; Adobe Illustrator, Adobe Photoshop

→   *Nina*, 2006, editorial and T-shirts design; Adobe Illustrator, Adobe Photoshop

→→ *Hippie girl*, 2007, JEM Sportswear, T-shirt; Adobe Illustrator, Adobe Photoshop

Mateu Velasco

lives and works in Rio de Janeiro (RJ), Brazil
www.mateuvelasco.com

↑ Portrait of unknown, 2009, personal work;
ink, watercolour and Adobe Photoshop

→ *Tattoo Boy*, 2010, personal work;
ink, watercolour and Adobe Photoshop

→→ *Polaroidz*, 2009, personal work;
ink, watercolour and Adobe Photoshop

Andrea Ventura

lives and works in New York (NY), USA
www.andreaventuraart.com

"Every portrait is also a self-portrait."

„*Jedes Porträt ist auch ein Selbstporträt.*"

«*Chaque portrait est aussi un autoportrait.*»

↑   Robert Johnson, 2001, Grove Press, book cover;
acrylic and charcoal on paper

→   Louis Armstrong, 2008, Italo Lupi Design, calendar;
acrylic and charcoal on paper

→→ Sean Connery in the role of 007, 2003, *Premiere*,
magazine article; acrylic and charcoal on paper

↑   Jean-Luc Godard, 2009, Rizzoli, book cover;
acrylic and charcoal on paper

→   Woody Allen, 2004, *Premiere*, magazine article;
acrylic and charcoal on paper

←← Ted Kennedy, 2009, *The New York Times*,
newspaper article; acrylic and charcoal on paper

→→ Muriel Spark, 2010,
Harper's magazine, article;
acrylic and charcoal on paper

↓   Zeno Strauss, 2005,
Canadian Business, magazine article;
acrylic and charcoal on paper

↑   Franz Kafka, 2005, personal work,
promotional; acrylic and charcoal on paper

→   Arthur Schopenhauer, 2009, Rizzoli,
book cover; acrylic and charcoal on paper

Raphaël Vicenzi

lives and works in Brussels, Belgium
www.mydeadpony.com

AGENT
Colagene
www.colagene.com

> *"I am trying to piece back the lost parts of myself through these portraits."*

> *„Ich versuche, durch diese Porträts meine verlorenen Anteile wieder zusammenzusetzen."*

> *« À travers ces portraits, j'essaie de retrouver des morceaux de moi-même que j'ai perdus. »*

↑   *Gloom is gold*, 2010, personal work;
Adobe Photoshop, Adobe Illustrator, watercolour

→   *A patient love*, 2010, personal work;
Adobe Photoshop, watercolour, markers

→→ *I so don't care*, 2010, personal work; Adobe
Photoshop, watercolour, markers, vintage source

↑ *Broken-hearted heroes*, 2009, personal work;
Adobe Photoshop, watercolour, markers

→ *Crying out rainbows*, 2010, personal work;
Adobe Photoshop, markers

←← *Wild Mother*, 2010, personal work;
Adobe Photoshop, Adobe Illustrator

Marco Wagner

lives and works in Veitshoechheim, Germany
www.marcowagner.net

AGENT

Jutta Fricke Illustrators
Germany
www.jutta-fricke.de

Jennifer Vaughn
San Francisco
www.jenvaughnart.com

"I love to do portraits and find the right techniques, colours, and media to emphasise the characteristics of a face."

„Ich liebe es, Porträts zu gestalten und die richtigen Techniken, Farben und Medien zu finden, um die Eigenarten eines Gesichts zu betonen."

« J'adore faire des portraits et trouver les techniques, couleurs et supports appropriés pour mettre en valeur les caractéristiques d'un visage. »

↑ *Bojovníci #1*, portrait of Muhammad Ali, 2009, 19Karen Exhibition Space; acrylic and papercuts on cardboard

→→ Pete Doherty, 2010, 19Karen Exhibition Space; acrylic and papercuts on cardboard

↑ Joachim Löw, 2010, *Gala Men*, magazine
article; hand drawing, Adobe Photoshop

←← *Banderillero*, 2009, Mark Murphy, exhibited
at Art Basel Miami 2009; acrylic on board

↑   Bob Dylan, 2010, 19Karen Exhibition Space;
acrylic, pen and papercuts on cardboard

↑ *Kooia*, 2010, personal work;
acrylic on board

← Elliott Smith, 2009, personal work;
pencil and crayon on cardboard

Frankie Watt

lives and works in North Vancouver (BC), Canada

AGENT
Folio
www.folioart.co.uk

> "My practice is to portray an individual's likeness and invoke a sense of quiet intimacy between the image and the viewer."

> „Wenn ich jemanden porträtiere, stelle ich das Konterfei eines Individuums dar und rufe eine Stimmung der stillen Intimität zwischen Bild und Betrachter hervor."

> « Dans mes portraits, je représente fidèlement le sujet et je crée un sentiment d'intimité tranquille entre l'image et le spectateur. »

↑ *Astronomer*, portrait of Sir Patrick Moore, 2001, personal work, private collection; featured in *The Lady* magazine and *The Evening Standard* newspaper in articles related to The Royal Society of Portrait Painters exhibition 2001; oil on board

→ *Head Study #1*, portrait of Prof. Simon Conway Morris, 2009, personal work, private collection; oil on board

→→ *Head Study #2*, portrait of Dr. Andrew Charles Elphinstone, 2010, personal work, private collection; oil on canvas

← *Winter in black and red*,
portrait of Winter Martini,
2010, personal work, private
collection; oil on canvas

↓ *Zoe H*, 2009, personal
work, private collection;
oil on canvas

↑ *Sarah H*, 2009, personal work,
private collection; oil on canvas

←← Nikki Roosen, 2010, personal
work, private collection; oil on canvas

↑   *Portrait of a young girl*, portrait of Lauren K.,
2009, personal work, exhibition; oil on board

→→ *Head of Young Boy*, portrait of Tad K., 2010,
personal work, private collection; oil on canvas

Silke Werzinger

lives and works in Berlin, Germany
www.colagene.com

AGENT
Colagene
www.colagene.com

"Faces and the stories they are able to tell are fascinating to me. When doing a portrait I am not finished until the person looks back at me."

„Gesichter und die Geschichten, die sie erzählen können, faszinieren mich. Wenn ich an einem Porträt arbeite, bin ich erst dann fertig, wenn mich die Person darin ansieht."

« Les visages et les histoires qu'ils sont capables de raconter me fascinent. Lorsque je fais un portrait, je n'ai terminé que lorsque l'image me regarde. »

↑   *Summer #3*, portrait of my friend Steffi, 2010, personal work, exhibition; hand drawing

→   *Men and beards*, portrait of Patrick Petitjean, 2009, *Maxi* magazine, editorial; hand drawing, collage

→→ Stephen Frears, 2010, *Premiere* magazine, editorial; hand drawing, collage

↑   *Little Sweethearts #2*, 2009, personal work;
hand drawing, Adobe Photoshop

↑ The Audience, 2009,
Hazelwood Vinyl Plastics,
CD; hand drawing

← *Men's bad conscience*,
2010, *Annabelle* magazine,
Switzerland, editorial;
hand drawing

Autumn Whitehurst

lives and works in Brooklyn (NY), USA
http://awhitehurst.com

AGENT

Art Department
New York
www.art-dept.com

Serlin Associates
London
www.serlinassociates.com

"I try to bring a bit of spirit and personality to the portrait and hope that for even just a moment some sort of an impression is being made."

„Ich versuche, dem Porträt ein wenig Geist und Persönlichkeit zu verleihen, und hoffe, dass eine Art von Eindruck möglich wird – und wenn auch nur für den Moment."

« J'essaie d'apporter un peu d'esprit et de personnalité au portrait, et j'espère que, même pour un bref moment, il laisse une sorte d'impression. »

↑   *Genomics*, 2007, *The Telegraph*, magazine article;
Adobe Photoshop, Adobe Illustrator, Corel Painter

→   *Blonde*, 2007, *The Telegraph*, magazine article;
Adobe Photoshop, Adobe Illustrator, Corel Painter

→→ *Winter*, 2006, *The Telegraph*, magazine article;
Adobe Photoshop, Adobe Illustrator, Corel Painter

↑   *Eating for Beauty*, 2008,
The Telegraph, magazine article;
Adobe Photoshop, Adobe Illustrator,
Corel Painter

→   *Lavender*, 2006, *The Telegraph*,
magazine article; Adobe Photoshop,
Adobe Illustrator, Corel Painter

←← *Stress*, 2006, *The Telegraph*,
magazine article, Adobe Photoshop,
Adobe Illustrator, Corel Painter

Dan Williams

lives and works in Glasgow, UK
www.dan-williams.net

AGENT
Lindgren & Smith
www.lindgrensmith.com

"These portraits are painted for **The Drawbridge** *directly from photographic reference – time, geography, and mortality don't allow otherwise."*

„Diese Porträts wurden für **The Drawbridge** *gemalt, und zwar direkt von einer Fotovorlage – Zeit, Ort und Sterblichkeit ließen nichts anderes zu."*

« Ces portraits sont peints pour **The Drawbridge** *directement à partir d'une photographie de référence – le temps, la géographie et la mortalité ne laissent pas d'autre choix. »*

↑   José Saramago, 2008, *The Drawbridge*;
ink and watercolour

→   Ryuichi Sakamoto, 2008, *The Drawbridge*;
ink and watercolour

→→ Roberto Saviano, 2010, *The Drawbridge*;
ink and watercolour

↑   Taryn Simon, 2007, *The Drawbridge*;
ink and watercolour

↗   Max Frisch, 2010, *The Drawbridge*;
ink and watercolour

→ Umberto Eco, 2007, *The Drawbridge*;
ink and watercolour

↓ Irvine Welsh, 2008, *The Drawbridge*;
ink and watercolour

Paul X. Johnson

lives and works in Newcastle, UK
http://paulxjohnson.com

AGENT
Folio
www.folioart.co.uk

> *"I love portraiture. When it comes to my art there's nothing in the world that is more interesting to me than human form, especially the face."*

> *„Ich liebe das Porträtieren. Wenn es um meine Kunst geht, gibt es nichts in der Welt, das für mich interessanter ist als die menschliche Gestalt, vor allem das Gesicht."*

> *« J'adore les portraits. En ce qui concerne la pratique de mon art, il n'y a rien en ce monde qui m'intéresse plus que la forme humaine, et particulièrement le visage. »*

↑ Daniel Day-Lewis as Daniel Plainview in the movie *There Will Be Blood*, 2010, personal work; mixed media

→ *Bones*, portrait of Anon., 2010, personal work; mixed media

→→ The character Rachael in the movie *Blade Runner*, 2010, personal work; mixed media

Index of subjects
Personenregister/Index des sujets

Acknowledgements / Danksagungen / Remerciements

First and foremost, my sincere thanks go to all the illustrators for supplying the most astonishing work and for constantly keeping in touch with us in order to improve the end result. This book is quite specific in its subject matter, and collaborating with over 80 illustrators was an immense pleasure. My other big thanks, of course, go to Daniel Siciliano Bretas, my right hand at TASCHEN headquarters in Cologne. Daniel worked tirelessly on the design and layout, paying meticulous attention to detail and delivering the final proofs in record time. I would also like to express my sincere gratitude to Steven Heller, who worked closely with us to select a truly diverse showcase of creative talent, as well as Kako, who has produced my portrait for the introduction. Their expertise was of the greatest importance for this publication, and their vast knowledge of illustration is unsurpassed. On our production front, Stefan Klatte has done an amazing job from beginning to end, and through his valiant efforts we were, as always, able to optimise each step of the production process, improving the quality along the way. I would also like to acknowledge all the illustrators' agents, who were always on hand to lend us their support.

Julius Wiedemann

← *Birds Watcher*, portrait of
Tippi Hedren by Tomer Hanuka,
2009, personal work; ink, digital

Imprint

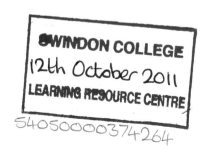

© 2011 TASCHEN GmbH
Hohenzollernring 53, D-50672 Köln
www.taschen.com

To stay informed about upcoming TASCHEN titles,
please request our magazine at www.taschen.com/magazine
or write to TASCHEN, Hohenzollernring 53, D-50672 Cologne,
Germany, contact@taschen.com, Fax: +49-221-254919.
We will be happy to send you a free copy of our magazine
which is filled with information about all of our books.

Page 002: *Jacko*, portrait of Michael Jackson by Hanoch Piven, 1995

Design and layout: Daniel Siciliano Bretas
Production: Stefan Klatte

Editor: Julius Wiedemann
Editorial Coordination: Daniel Siciliano Bretas

English Revision: Chris Allen
German Translation: Jürgen Dubau
French Translation: Aurélie Daniel for Equipo de Edición

Printed in Italy
ISBN 978-3-8365-2425-4